KT-213-131

research

TEACH YOURSELF BOOKS

research

Paul Oliver

TEACH YOURSELF BOOKS

A catalogue record for this title is available from The British Library

ISBN 0 340 69081 X

First published 1997
Impression number 10 9 8   7 6   5 4 3 2 1
Year   2002 2001 2000 1999 1998 1997

The 'Teach Yourself' name and logo are registered trade marks of
Hodder & Stoughton Ltd.

Copyright © 1997 Paul Oliver

All rights reserved. No part of this publication may be reproduced or transmitted in
any form or by any means, electronic or mechanical, including photocopy, recording,
or any information storage and retrieval system, without permission in writing from
the publisher or under licence from the Copyright Licensing Agency Limited.
Further details of such licences (for reprographic reproduction) may be obtained
from the Copyright Licensing Agency Limited, of 90 Tottenham Court Road,
London W1P 9HE.

Typeset by Transet Limited, Coventry, England.
Printed in Great Britain for Hodder & Stoughton Educational, a division of
Hodder Headline Plc, 338 Euston Road, London NW1 3BH by Cox and Wyman Ltd,
Reading, Berks.

CONTENTS

Foreword

FOREWORD

The purpose of this book is to help you plan and carry out research projects. You may have to design an investigation at work, whether in industry or commerce, and plan a suitable way of collecting data. Alternatively, you could be asked to report on the effectiveness of a new development, and feel that a small research study would be a good way of doing this. *Teach Yourself Research* will help you to get started and to see the research through to the final report.

The book is also designed to help you with university courses in which you have to complete a research study or dissertation. It provides advice on choosing the appropriate methodology and on analysing your data. It is written to be of help up to, and including, postgraduate-level study.

The message behind this book is that research is a fascinating, practical activity, in which many people can be involved. If you want to investigate an issue in a systematic, logical way, then I hope that you will find this book a useful guide.

Enjoy your research!

Paul Oliver

INTRODUCTION TO
RESEARCH

1

THE NATURE OF RESEARCH

Everyone does research

Research is a term which we hear used quite frequently, and it normally conjures up an image of laboratories and precise, scientific work. It is easy to be impressed by the idea of research. We might easily assume that research can only be carried out by a few highly qualified 'experts', and that the activity is beyond the reach of everyday life. One of the main purposes of this book is to explain the procedures of research in a straightforward way, and also to suggest that many of us are either involved in activities bordering on research, or can easily start it. The word 'research' can be used in a great many different situations, and it may help to start by looking at the concept, and the ways in which it is used.

First of all, research is about advancing knowledge and understanding. However, it does not necessarily have to involve a dramatic discovery or breakthrough in scientific knowledge. Research often involves rather ordinary and unexciting activities, and proceeds in small stages rather than in great leaps. Research may indeed solve a complex problem which has been causing confusion for ages, but it will more likely simply shed a little light on a problematic area. It is perhaps rather too much to hope for that research will always solve our problems. Medical researchers, for example, often have to struggle with finding a cure for an illness, slowly piecing together fragments of data, and never knowing quite whether all the evidence will fit together to provide a solution to the problem.

It is important that we do not expect too much of research. To the uninitiated, research can sound very complex and sophisticated, as if it were a panacea for all ills. In fact, we would probably be wise to be rather more modest about its possible gains. Much research involves taking data which has been collected previously under a variety of circumstances, and then collecting more data under similar situations in order to check the results. Such research can sometimes either affirm or call into question the reliability of the original data. A motor-vehicle technician trying to establish the cause of a fault in a car engine goes through a process such as this. Data is collected from one car, and this may suggest a specific cause for the fault. Whenever data is available from another similar vehicle, the evidence will be crosschecked with the first car.

Sometimes research takes a general theory and then attempts to apply it in particular circumstances. Other research involves analysing ideas and concepts in order to explore the precision with which they are used. In fact, an important aspect of all research is that ideas should be expressed very clearly. Without precision of thought and expression, it is not easy to draw useful conclusions in research.

Research activities, then, can be extremely varied, although they do share some basic characteristics. It is possible to use the term 'research' simply in connection with the data-collection phase of an inquiry. However, we normally use the term to refer to the entire process of data collection, data analysis and the drawing of conclusions. We therefore tend to assume that research will result in a new viewpoint on a subject, or that we will be able to think about something in a fresh way. If research is particularly comprehensive and detailed, then it may result in the generation of a theory, or a general statement which is relevant to a wide variety of situations. Psychologists who have studied human behaviour may produce a theory which attempts to describe and explain the reasons for people behaving in certain ways. Such a theory may perhaps be used to try to explain the behaviour of different individuals from those originally studied.

Most research is of the type which is based upon very accurate observations. Images come to mind of a scientist in a laboratory taking precise readings with a measuring instrument; of an astronomer measuring the position of a newly discovered star; or of an environmentalist testing for chemicals in a river. All of these kinds of observation probably involve the collection of numerical measurements, but research does not necessarily involve a mathematical approach. Very often it involves collecting data in the form of words alone. We might want, for example, to investigate the behaviour of certain groups of people, and might keep notes on our observations. Another important form of data used in research are conversational records. Discussions and conversations are recorded, and are then carefully written out or transcribed. Whether the data involves mathematical measurements or verbal records of some kind, such data is collected by using our senses, such as sight and hearing. This kind of data is given the name 'empirical' data.

Many of us regularly collect this kind of information in our everyday lives, although we probably do not think of it as 'research'. People who work in a business or provide a public service often keep records of the number of customers or clients they have had. They frequently analyse these records to see if there are any fluctuations. They want to know if their business is doing well, or if there has been a decline in the number of clients. Businesses could not manage for long without keeping accurate sales figures and marketing information. This data is regularly analysed, not only to make sure that the business is solvent, but to look for developing trends.

If you work in education, you will be all too familiar with the need to monitor student numbers. Most educational institutions, from schools to universities, receive a level of funding which depends upon the number of students which they can manage to recruit. Trends in student recruitment are therefore followed very carefully. Institutions also collect data on the number of students who leave their courses early. This information is usually in a numerical form. However, colleges and universities are also interested in the reasons for students leaving. They usually try to collect information on this by sending questionnaires to students, or by interviewing students who are leaving, and this data is clearly in verbal form.

Many people collect empirical data not as part of their job, but for a hobby or spare-time interest. The investigation of local and family history is a popular interest, and this involves collecting a lot of research data. This kind of empirical data may come from old newspapers and archives, from parish records, from libraries, and also from talking to people. Elderly people are a very interesting source of historical data about past events, and often enjoy talking about the world in which they lived as a child. People involved in local-history societies are very much concerned with collecting empirical data, in much the same way as professional historians.

Sometimes, however, research is based less upon observational data and more upon the way in which we use concepts and ideas. Empirical data can, on occasions, only take us part of the way in a research investigation. For example, suppose that a group of social workers is planning ways of helping the elderly in society. They may start by collecting empirical data on the number of elderly people in a community, and on factors such as income and housing. However, when they start to translate that data into practical policies for helping the elderly, they will almost certainly begin to ask themselves questions such as:

- Is this the right kind of policy to have?
- Should we have this kind of housing provision?
- Is this level of financial help fair to people?

These kinds of question depend very much upon knowing what we mean by words like right and fair. We all know that people do not have identical views about what it means to be fair. The only way in which these matters can be resolved is to think very carefully about the concepts, and to consider their meaning within this particular context. This process is known as **conceptual analysis**, or philosophical analysis.

Empirical research and conceptual analysis usually go hand in hand. In any research investigation, it is important to start by thinking clearly about the concepts being used, and about any special meaning which they might acquire in that particular context. In addition, when we draw conclusions from research, we often employ words like 'should' and 'ought' to reflect our own feelings about research recommendations. It is important to be clear about how these words reflect our own possible opinions and preconceptions.

— Research as systematic enquiry —

Another characteristic of research is that it is typically very ordered and systematic. A researcher tries to approach an issue in a very logical way, moving step by step through a carefully planned research design. The stages of the research design are each carefully thought out in order to choose the best means of data collection and analysis. The starting point for research is usually to think of the aims which are hoped to be achieved. From these aims stem the most appropriate sampling approach, data-collection method, and process of data analysis. All these issues are collectively known as the research **methodology**.

Perhaps this is what distinguishes the general collection of information from genuine research. If someone goes to their local library to collect information on a topic, then we would not normally describe that as research. If, however, there is a systematic approach to solving a particular problem, and if there are a series of planned stages to the investigation, then this is much closer to being research.

When carrying out an inquiry, the researcher tries not to let personal bias or a personal belief-system enter into the way in which the research is conducted. The researcher tries to construct the research design in a balanced and disinterested way. Once agreed upon, the research design controls the way in which the research is carried out. There is a consistent attempt to avoid personal involvement and subjectivity, but rather to make the research process as objective as possible.

Of course, it is very easy to let personal feelings creep into an investigation. If, for example, you are carrying out some market research to find out how satisfied people are with your product, you obviously want them to say complimentary things about it. There is a temptation to ask **leading questions**, inviting people to make supportive comments. If the research is to be of value, however, all of these temptations should be avoided, and personal involvement should be removed as far as possible from the inquiry.

Research is very much concerned with the general application of its results. Researchers are rarely satisfied if the results of an investigation can only be applied to the case or sample studied in the particular research project. In an ideal world, they would like to be able to apply the results in as wide a context as possible. In particular, the purpose of much research is to create general principles which can be seen to be relevant elsewhere. Such principles can ultimately be developed into theories.

Finally, the significant aspect of the results of research is that they are normally published, or at least disseminated among a community of researchers, academics and fellow professionals. This tradition is very important for research. On the one hand, it puts the research into the public domain, and makes it available for critical scrutiny. Our peers can evaluate the results, and decide whether they feel that the data justifies the conclusions which have been drawn. Even if no one ever examines the research, the crucial thing is that it is actually available for scrutiny. The second important aspect of publication is that someone can replicate the research and try to obtain the same results. This is a check upon both the reliability of the research and the care taken when collecting the original data.

Research, then, takes many forms, but it generally includes some of the following important characteristics:

- the investigation of a new issue;
- a systematic research design;
- a rationale for the collection and analysis of data;
- an attempt at **generalisation** using the results;
- an effort to be as objective as possible;
- the dissemination of results.

Investigations do not need to be carried out in a university or a large research institute in order to fulfil these characteristics. Obviously, a lot of research is of this nature, but small-scale, everyday enquiry carried out in a systematic way can be fairly described as research, if it tries to meet these kinds of criteria. A useful discussion of the concept of research can be found in Hughes (1980, p.11; see the 'Further reading' section).

—— Scientific basis of research ——

The fact that the term social 'science' is used at all, illustrates one of the main viewpoints of the way in which research involving human beings and human societies should proceed. This is that there should be no fundamental difference between the way in which knowledge is accumulated in subjects such as physics and chemistry, and the way in which investigations are conducted in studies of people and societies. **Positivism** (a term first used by the French philosopher Auguste Comte) is the name for the belief that the methodology of the natural sciences, such as physics, should be used in sociology, psychology and other human sciences, collectively known as **social sciences**. The belief of positivists is that the natural sciences have evolved an approach to research which can be applied universally, and which gives rise better than any other approach to new knowledge and insights.

Research in the natural sciences tends to proceed according to certain beliefs about the way in which research should be conducted, and in the systems that govern the world. One of the basic beliefs is in the idea of cause and effect, or that every observable event has a specific cause. An everyday example is that a ball moves across a football field because someone has kicked it. Alternatively, in a laboratory, a spring is seen to extend more and more when heavier weights are attached to the end of it. These may seem such obvious statements about how the world works that they are scarcely worth recording. However, while in a laboratory experiment this idea of cause and effect may seem clear and measurable, it is less easy to demonstrate in studies involving human beings. Imagine, for example, asking yourself why you behaved in a certain way to someone else. There may have been many factors which affected your behaviour. You might find it very difficult to pin down your behaviour simply to one cause. You may even find it difficult to work out any reason for a particular piece of behaviour. Human behaviour and interaction is so much more complex than laboratory experiments that it is very difficult to reduce it to the level of one cause determining one effect.

Looking at things in terms of causes and effects is sometimes called 'determinism'. One cannot say that social scientists are never interested in trying to find causal relationships, but rather that they generally feel that the issues which they are investigating are much more complex and often require approaches other than positivism.

Another major feature of natural science is that it is normally concerned with precise measurement, and indeed we associate laboratories with dials, measuring instruments and computers. It would seem a rather strange physics experiment if we simply said that a spring got longer when greater weights were attached to it, rather than measuring how much it extended. The whole focus of natural science is to take accurate measurements, and to try to say how much one factor has changed when something else has affected it. Science, then, is concerned with quantification.

To a certain extent this is also true of social-science disciplines. When sociologists are studying unemployment, they usually want to know how many people are out of work in a particular week, rather than only having a general idea of the figure. Some branches of psychology are very much concerned with the measurement of human abilities, such as intelligence, or of qualities such as introversion or extroversion, and tests are used to try to give a numerical value to these. On the other hand, there are many aspects of social science which clearly do not lend themselves to quantification. If we are researching people's attitudes to things, it is very difficult to consider giving them a numerical value alone. Most researchers would try to obtain some kind of verbal or written account of attitudes, in addition to any attempt to obtain a numerical evaluation of them.

Scientific research is not simply interested in the results of the particular experiment being carried out at the time, but also in how well those results can be applied to other, similar situations. For example, if adding a particular weight doubles the length of a spring, the physicist would want to know whether all springs behaved in this way. The physicist might ask such questions as whether the extension depends upon:

- the tightness of the coils of the spring;
- the substance of which the spring is made;
- the original length of the spring.

All of these factors could affect the extension of a spring. In research terms, they are called '**variables**'. They are qualities of the spring which might 'vary' under different circumstances, and hence affect the spring's length.

In cases such as this, there would have to be many experiments carried out with different types of spring before any conclusions could be reached. Eventually, it might be possible to predict with some confidence how other springs would behave when weights were attached to them. This ability to conduct experiments, and then to apply the results to a number of other situations, is called 'generalisation'. The capacity to generalise is regarded as being a very important aspect of natural science.

In social science, however, it is much less easy to generalise, because of the enormous variations in the human population. It is possible to mass-produce a large number of very similar springs, and to be fairly sure that they will all behave in the same way when weights are attached to them. However, human beings are so different that we cannot make the same assumptions.

In many situations in social-science research, we have to be satisfied with studying a single social situation, and not worrying too much about how typical it is. Sometimes it is enough to leave the reader to decide the extent to which the research can be applied elsewhere. This is particularly true of so-called '**case study**' research, in which a particular individual or organisation is studied as a special case. In situations such as these, the purpose of the research is to gather in-depth information about the particular case being studied. Sometimes, however, social-science research does attempt to gener-alise. This is particularly true of **survey** research, in which a sample is taken from a large number of potential individuals or situations being studied.

The final characteristic of the scientific approach is that of trying to establish general **laws**, or theories, which are useful in helping to predict future events. Some of the most straightforward examples come from introductory physics. Boyle's Law, for instance, describes the relationship between the volume and pressure of a given mass of gas at constant temperature. The law is very effective at predicting what will happen to a quantity of gas when the pressure is increased. It not only tells you that the volume will decrease, but it will allow you to calculate by how much this will happen. What is more, the law does not apply only to one gas, but to all gases. It is therefore very generalisable. One of the main purposes of scientific research is to express results in the form of 'laws', which are straightforward state-ments of the relationship between variables, and which enable accur-ate predictions to be made.

Most scientists, however, want to go one step further, and to develop a 'theory'. In a sense, the theory is even more general that the law. Not only does it predict future events, but it provides an explanation of the observed relationships between variables. A related example to that of Boyle's Law is the Kinetic Theory of Gases. This theory explains the behaviour of gases not merely in response to pressure changes, but also in relation to changes in other variables, such as temperature. The theory does this by proposing that the behaviour of gases can best be understood in terms of the movement of the gas molecules. This theory is very good at both explaining the behaviour of gases, and at predicting their future behaviour in relation to changed variables.

Such laws and theories have a simplicity, a predictive accuracy, and a generalisability which make them very attractive in a natural-science research context. In social science, however, it is much more difficult to construct laws and theories which explain and predict human behaviour. To take a rather absurd example, suppose that we tried to investigate the effect of temperature upon human behaviour, much as we might try to investigate the effect of temperature upon a chemical reaction. As the weather became hotter, we might observe some people becoming more irritable, and others becoming calmer; some might become more physically active, while others might become more sleepy. It is difficult to imagine that we could construct a law or theory to explain the diversity of such observations. Such is the range of behaviour in human beings that it is difficult to explain it in terms of generalised statements.

Moreover, natural science rests on the assumption that there are observable facts which can be measured and analysed. In social science, it is much more difficult to accept the idea of 'social facts'. If we consider a 'social fact' such as 'unemployment rate', it is not quite the same kind of 'fact' as the rate of a chemical reaction. Unemployment is a difficult term to define precisely, and this results in considerable difficulty when it comes to measuring it. Unemployment might include, for example, people doing temporary work, voluntary work, or part-time work. It is thus not necessarily a clear-cut concept. Unemployment can also be due to a number of factors, such as being sacked, being made redundant, or leaving work voluntarily. It is not a concept which lends itself to precise measurement in the same way as the data in a chemistry laboratory.

The difficulty in defining precisely measurable social facts makes it difficult to accept the notion of the objective observer in social science. Much more common is the idea of the researcher as being a participant in a situation. Rather than standing back and collecting data impartially, the researcher is seen as being more involved in the social process, and as an interpreter of social events.

An additional focus of social-science research is to try to reveal the ways in which people make sense of the world. In this case, it is not only important to collect accurate observations of human behaviour, but also to seek to explore the ways in which individuals build up a view of the world. It is not easy to do this, because we cannot peer inside people's minds. We do, however, have data regarding the kind of language that people use, and the expressions which they employ to try to explain the world. In addition, we can examine interactive behaviour between individuals, and the way in which people construct a common meaning for events.

The nature of social science is discussed in Mann (1985, p.16; see the 'Further reading' section).

——— Developing a hypothesis ———

One of the main characteristics of research is that it is a very systematic activity. Data is collected in order to test a particular problem; the data is analysed, and conclusions are then drawn. The crucial starting point for research is to have an issue to investigate. In the scientific tradition, this issue is normally expressed in the form of a **hypothesis**. This is a clear statement, which expresses an assumption about the research issue, and is sufficiently precise to test. The easiest way to explain this is to consider an example of a hypothesis, as follows.

Hypothesis
The greater the degree of democratic decision-making in a commercial organisation, then the greater the level of employee job satisfaction.

This hypothesis takes two basic ideas – 'democratic decision-making' and 'employee job satisfaction' – and suggests that they are connected. Some organisations are controlled by the central management team, others have varying degrees of employee participation. Equally, there are clearly varying degrees of employee job satisfaction. The hypothesis above suggests that the two variables are connected, to the extent that as one increases then the other increases as well. This can be stated in more mathematical terms as one variable being directly proportional to the other.

Although there are two variables in the above hypothesis, they are connected in such a way that one variable is claimed to affect the other. It is suggested that job satisfaction is affected by the extent of democratic decision-making. Job satisfaction is therefore termed the **dependent variable**, and decision-making the **independent variable**.

Hypotheses can be derived in a variety of ways. You could, for example, observe a social situation and come to a conclusion about some of the variables which are operating within it. You could then develop some hypotheses which connect two or more of these variables. Alternatively, you might take an existing theory which has been developed by someone else, and use that to produce further hypotheses.

The main requirement is that hypotheses should fulfil certain criteria. Firstly, they should be precisely worded. The variables should be clear and understandable, and the proposed relationship between them should be articulated. Secondly, the hypothesis should state the conditions and circumstances under which it is supposed to apply. For example, the hypothesis on decision-making is set within the context of a 'commercial' organisation. This may or may not be sufficiently precise, depending upon one's viewpoint, but it is an attempt to set the proposed relationship within certain parameters.

The hypothesis should also be capable of being tested empirically. It is very important that a researcher is clear as to the grounds on which it should be judged. This applies not only to the person who developed the hypothesis, but also to other researchers who might find themselves gathering data in order to evaluate it. The hypothesis should be phrased in such a way that it is clear what sort of data needs to be collected, and how it should be analysed in order to either support or refute the hypothesis.

—— Primary and secondary data ——

Researchers tend to think of data as being in different categories, and two of the most basic categories are those of primary and secondary data. **Primary data** is normally regarded as being data which is collected by the original researcher who is using it for an investigation. **Secondary data** is data which has been collected by someone else for a separate purpose, and is then used by the researcher.

However, the problem with definitions is that we can sometimes think of exceptions. Sometimes a researcher may employ a group of people to act as data collectors, or perhaps to administer a questionnaire. Although the researcher has not collected the data personally, it can still be regarded as primary data; it remains data which has been collected for a specific purpose as outlined by the researcher. On the other hand, suppose that you use data which has been collected for a separate research study with a different purpose, and that you analyse it from your own point of view. Although it is still research data, it should probably be regarded as secondary data, because it was not collected according to your specifications. The boundary between primary and secondary data is thus a little blurred, but the spirit of the distinction is sufficiently clear for practical purposes, and indeed raises some interesting sociological issues.

These issues derive mainly from the nature of the two types of data. Figure 1.1 gives examples of primary and secondary data. It should be noted, however, that the data types listed under primary data could be regarded as being secondary data if a different researcher chose to use the data for a new purpose. The data listed as secondary would not normally constitute primary data, except in certain situations, for example, if someone wrote an **autobiography** and later analysed it as data.

Primary data	Secondary data
Surveys	Autobiographies
Case studies	Government or other official statistics
Interview recordings	Records of business transactions
Experimental data	Legal documents
Observations	Journalism
Field notes	TV, radio or film

Figure 1.1 Types of primary and secondary data

These lists are not exhaustive, but should give an impression of the characteristics of the two categories.

The main advantage of primary data is that you, the researcher, control the data-collection process. You plan the research; you decide on the format of the questionnaire or the interview; you decide how to record the data; and you decide how to analyse it. This means that when you write up the research you are in a position to provide a detailed report which lists and explains both the presuppositions of the research and the particular perspective within which the data was analysed. This is a major advantage when writing a research report, but it also means that you may be expected to account for any disadvantages in the data, or in the research design.

On the other hand, if you are using secondary data for research purposes, you can almost never really understand the full circumstances behind the research design and the collection of the data. This is particularly true of official statistics. Consider the example of a school or college that keeps registers of students' attendance. Students who are late for class may well be recorded as such, but the final data will not reveal that element of discretion among the teachers as to whether or not to record someone as being late. The same applies to absentee records. A student may attend school in the morning and be marked present, but may not attend in the afternoon, or for part of the afternoon. The register system would have to be sufficiently precise to record this.

A different problem applies to marriage statistics. These cannot include the many couples who live together in a stable relationship and yet remain legally unmarried. Similarly, divorce statistics cannot include the marriages which have, to all intents and purposes, broken down, but whose partners have not legally dissolved the relationship.

If you use secondary data, it is therefore important to acknowledge that because it has been collected for one purpose, and in a particular way, it may omit certain categories of information. It is also important to try to understand the definitions used by the person who collected the original data. For example, in terms of data about full-time students, it would be important to know the distinction between a 'part-time' student, who studied for say, 18 hours each week, and a 'full-time' student, who studied for the same number of hours. The nature of the final data depends very much upon the original definitions which were used in the research design.

One advantage of using secondary data is that it often saves a great deal of time in terms of data collection. It would take a researcher a lot of effort to collect the type of statistical data which is normally found in government reports. Although they have the drawbacks discussed above, this saving of time can often be a great advantage.

Quantitative and qualitative methods

Another traditional means of distinguishing between types of data and also approaches to research is to think of them as involving either a quantitative or qualitative approach. Quantitative research seeks to collect data which is in a numerical form, and which can be analysed or presented using tables or charts of figures, histograms, graphs, or statistics. **Qualitative data**, on the other hand, consists either of written or spoken words, and does not normally include any numerical measurements. Such data can consist of autobiographical accounts, **observation studies** and interviews.

Not only do these two categories represent very different types of data, but also quite different perspectives on the research process. **Quantitative data** is very much associated with the positivist approach to research, while qualitative methods are connected with an **interpretive approach**. The latter term can be used to refer to a range of approaches and perspectives in social science, including **ethnographic research** and interactionist methods. Essentially, the interpretive approach suggests that the positivists are wrong when they seek to collect 'factual' data in societies. Interpretive sociology suggests that external events in society can be understood in different ways by different people, and that this should be taken into account when gathering data. In many cases, human beings, unlike members of the inanimate world, can chose how they will respond to a particular stimulus. This makes the study of human society much more complex, and interactionists suppose that any research which fails to take into account the ways in which people make sense of the world is presenting an incomplete picture.

There can be a tendency for some researchers to view themselves as being either quantitative or qualitative researchers. However, it is often a sensible approach to try to incorporate both strategies into a research design, using what are sometimes called 'multiple methods', which can often help to provide a more detailed picture of the research topic than would otherwise be the case.

Lewins (1992, p.41; see the 'Further reading' section) provides a useful discussion of the nature of quantitative and qualitative approaches.

NEW CONCEPTS

Autobiography
Case study
Conceptual analysis
Dependent variable
Empirical
Ethnographic research
Generalisation
Hypothesis
Independent variable
Interpretive approaches
Laws

Leading questions
Methodology
Observation studies
Positivism
Primary data
Qualitative data
Quantitative data
Secondary data
Social sciences
Survey
Variable

2

THE USES OF RESEARCH

Clear description

Perhaps the most basic use of research is to provide a clear description of phenomena. We often observe events in everyday life without really 'looking' and 'seeing' clearly. Perhaps understandably, we often miss the minutiae of events because we are preoccupied, or do not train ourselves to be observant. We tend to 'see' either what is significant at the time, or what we want to see, or else what we have time to see. This results in an incomplete picture, upon which it is very difficult to base conclusions. Precise observation and description are the basis of research.

The limitations which tend to be inherent in everyday observation sometimes cause discussion and problem evaluation between people to be flawed, because they are based on erroneous data. This is as much true in the workplace as it is in everyday life. What we tend to regard as being scientific thinking is based upon clear, careful and precise observation, which is also well documented.

Consider the case of animal behaviour. Before field biologists can begin to understand why animals behave as they do, they first have to collect a large amount of descriptive data in which they can search for behavioural patterns. Many people, for example, enjoy ornithology as a hobby, and take pleasure in watching birds in their natural habitats. While the interest remains at this level it is recreational, but if detailed observations are kept in a log, then it starts to assume the first characteristics of research. When watching a species of waterfowl on a lake we might start to keep systematic records by asking such questions as:

- Do the birds always swim in the middle of the lake, or do they sometimes come to the edge?
- Do they totally submerge themselves when feeding?
- How long do their dives last?
- Does the species mix with other species?
- What is their flight pattern like?
- How frequently do they fly when they are not disturbed?

Observations and answers to questions such as these, would help in building up a picture of the species within its environment.

Another area in which detailed research observations are very valuable, is in the study of human organisations. Most of us are part of one organisation or another, and yet most of the time we are preoccupied with our own, specific function within it. This can be very true of people in work organisations. Only when we have the opportunity to conduct observational research do we start to get a feeling for the totality of the organisation. We begin to feel a sense of:

- social and friendship patterns;
- attempts by individuals or groups to achieve power or status;
- patterns of decision-making;
- networks of communication.

Observational research is very useful when applied to social groups whose behaviour is covert, or not fully understood. This may be because the group exhibits aspects of deviant behaviour, for example. It is very difficult to understand the culture of groups such as drug-takers, football hooligans, or those involved in vandalism, without careful observational data. Once such data is available, it may be possible to construct a picture of the values and norms of the group and, if necessary, develop a strategy to help or rehabilitate them.

A final example of the use of clear description and observation is in the investigation of major accidents involving train or plane crashes. Such investigations have a great deal in common with academic research. The first stage is in the meticulous gathering of fragments from the crash scene, and in collecting first-person accounts from those involved, or from witnesses. Only when this time-consuming task is completed do the investigators start to develop possible explanations for the crash.

Understanding why events happen

Once we have a very clear description of events in the world, then the next stage is to try to understand why and how they happen. We might seek answers to questions such as:

How does a new drug manage to cure an illness? What is the actual biochemical mechanism at work?

or

Why do certain individuals commit violently criminal acts?

Much of scientific research has always been concerned with establishing general laws which govern and describe patterns of events. Such laws are sometimes very well known, such as that of gravity, but at other times they simply summarise a range of empirical findings which always appear to be true, and which include every known instance of an event.

In the example of the medical treatment mentioned in the question above, it may be that in each observed incidence of an illness a particular enzematic malfunction is noticed. The enzyme has a small group of molecules missing, which prevents it interacting with its substrate chemical. Thus the enzyme may not facilitate the correct metabolic reaction of the body. The 'treatment' chemical can generate the missing molecules, which then attach themselves to the enzyme, with the result that the effects of the illness are removed. The explanation of the remedy is in terms of the universal nature of the observation of the enzymatic malfunction. If this type of situation can be understood at the molecular level, then it provides a fairly clear instance of scientific explanation.

Explanation and understanding in the social sciences is not quite as straightforward as this medical example. The reason for this is that in the study of human behaviour it is rarely possible to develop statements which describe it in terms of all instances. There is not the same degree of regularity and predictability in human behaviour as is normally found in, say, chemical reactions. It has always been very difficult, for example, to understand the causes of criminal behaviour.

Some people have suggested that criminality is a result of environmental factors, such as a deprived upbringing, or of contact with criminal elements during childhood and adolescence. While this may be true in some cases, there are also many instances of individuals with deprived backgrounds who grow up to contribute positively to society. Another possible explanation for criminality is that there might exist some form of genetic inclination towards antisocial behaviour. According to this explanation, individuals may inherit a propensity for criminal behaviour and, almost irrespective of their environment, will be likely to exhibit such types of behaviour. Genetic explanations of behaviour such as this tend, however, to ignore the important element of human autonomy and free will. In other words, we may all inherit inclinations towards many types of behaviour, but that does not mean that we give in to our inclinations. When confronted with a situation, we can chose how to respond, and the way in which we react is often affected by what we have learned from our environment.

The relative influence of genetic and environmental factors has been a long-standing debate within the human sciences, and it seems clear that it is not simply a matter of chosing one explanation or another. Probably a better way of looking at the issue is to think of inherited and environmental factors as being in a constant state of interaction, and to regard both as having an effect upon individual behaviour.

However, although explanation is difficult enough in the natural sciences, and even more so in the social sciences, this does not prevent us from aspiring to a degree of understanding in most research activity. Humans have an almost unquenchable desire to make sense of, and to understand, the phenomena with which we are surrounded, and the limitations of our techniques are unlikely to deter us from the continuing search.

— Explaining organisational trends —

One of the main aims of research is to try to understand and explain organisational patterns and behaviour. Such organisational trends can be seen at the **macro level** of multinational companies, or of government departments; at the other extreme, they can be seen at the level of small companies, schools, clubs or societies. Managers of organisations are usually very interested in the way in which policy decisions have an effect on both the internal and the external environment of the organisation. A major purpose of research is to try to monitor and explain trends. For example, at government or government-department level, trends which might be of interest include:

- changes in home-ownership patterns in the population;
- trends in the use of public transport;
- employment changes in relation to variables such as age or gender;
- changes in the relationship between qualification level and **mean** income of individuals;
- productivity levels of different industries.

Ministers will naturally be very interested in explaining such trends in terms of changes in government policy, particularly if the changes are congruent with government predictions. On a smaller level, commercial companies are usually interested in such features as:

- changes in consumer demand for a product;
- effects of changes in manufacturing technology upon productivity;
- changes in transport facilities which might affect the price of raw materials, or of distribution costs for products;
- effects of new training programmes for staff upon the quality of products;
- demographic trends which might affect their marketing niche.

Such trends are potentially very complex to analyse. While someone working within the company may have a hunch about a particular change and the effect it may be having, the only reliable way in which to monitor the trend is to conduct a research investigation. There is really no short cut to obtaining accurate data and precise analysis. It takes time and commitment, but the results will be much more valid and useful than some assumptions made in haste.

Service industries are also very interested in monitoring trends, particularly in situations in which they receive an element of public funding. The following types of trend may be very susceptible to research investigations:

- changes in the number of clients helped per unit of expenditure;
- changes in the types and characteristics of clients;
- apparent changes in the life chances of clients as a result of the service provided;
- effects of different strategies for contacting clients;
- public perceptions of the utility and value of the service provided.

As discussed in the previous section, it is very difficult to provide absolute explanations for organisational trends which involve human beings, but organisations will always be interested in trends and their effects, and in implications that they may have for future policies.

There is always likely to be a dynamic equilibrium between policy changes and organisational trends. Research forms the primary tool with which managers can try to understand trends and hence develop new policies.

—— Predicting future developments ——

Prediction is one of the primary functions of research. Indeed it is difficult to imagine our current existence without the advantages brought about by accurate prediction based upon empirical evidence.

When we are driving, for example, we spend a great deal of time collecting data on the performance of the car that we own; on road conditions; on the behaviour of other motorists in certain situations; and on variations in traffic. We are amassing this data in our minds all the time, and draw upon it when we need to make a decision about how to drive. In effect, we accumulate a mental database, and analyse the data contained within it when we are confronted with an unusual situation. In winter in particular, when there can be ice and snow on the roads, we are usually very observant regarding the performance of the car, and especially of the tyres. We note the behaviour of the tyres under dry, wet, icy, slushy and snowy conditions, and all of this data is analysed when we set out in the morning. The analysis of this data affects our decisions about how hard to brake at corners, and about the speed at which we feel it is safe to travel. Of course, we do not always make the correct decisions, and unfortunately accidents result. However, driving would certainly become a much more dangerous and risky activity if it were not for our ability to collect empirical data, and to make predictions based upon that data. Research can be regarded as simply a formalisation and extension of this type of thought process.

A researcher working on aspects of road transport would probably tend to collect rather more data under a variety of road conditions, tyre pressures, tyre-tread patterns and speed, and such data would be formally recorded in some way. In research, there would also be a tendency to try to quantify data: for example, the magnitude of the frictional forces between tyre and road surface. Although a researcher would probably seek more data and quantitative measurements, the essence of the procedure would be the same. A discussion of prediction in social science can be found in Sayer (1993, p.130; see the 'Further reading' section).

The predictive process in research depends very much upon establishing accurate **causal connections**. Let us suppose that on every occasion event A is observed, then event B subsequently happens. We may feel that we are provisionally entitled to assume that when A occurs next, B will happen. If we are correct, then there may well be a causal connection, i.e. A causes B to occur. However, we cannot be absolutely sure about this, as there may well be a hitherto unknown influence which causes A, and also causes B a few moments later.

The clarification of these kinds of prediction works most effectively when there are fewer peripheral variables or, we might say, when the research situation is fairly simple and straightforward. When there are many possible variables it is usually much more difficult to predict with certainty that A is caused by B. To take an example, it may be observed that whenever there is a decline in the number of permanent jobs available in the economy the number of young people applying for educational and training courses increases. It may be considered that one causes the other, on the grounds that students study in order to develop the skills to get a job. On the other hand, a fall in jobs may have no noticeable effect on applications to college and university because young people may become disenchanted about the benefits of studying in terms of getting a job. Nevertheless, it is easy to think of a number of important activities in society,which would be very difficult to put into practice without the use of prediction based upon accurate data:

- an engineer would find it very difficult to design and construct a bridge without the benefit of predictions based upon known load-bearing capacities and the tensile-strengths of materials;
- psychologists would be unable to estimate some types of human potential without the help of predictions based upon the results of psychometric tests;
- meteorologists would be unable to judge weather trends without referring to predictions based upon extensive data collection from, for example, satellite photographs;

- doctors would be unlikely to be able to advise on the likely spread of an infectious disease without the use of predictions based upon knowledge of the particular organism and previous cases of infection.

It would be very difficult to make valid and reliable predictions of this type without the knowledge derived from careful and systematic research. Of course, we do not need what we call 'research' in order to acquire knowledge. This can still be gained in an *ad hoc* and incidental manner, but the knowledge thus obtained is likely to be piecemeal and uncoordinated.

Such a casual approach to the acquisition of knowledge can sometimes result in explanations which are based upon personal intuition or prejudice. Such explanations may or may not be correct, but research provides us with a systematic mechanism for testing such beliefs. Research may not always provide us with the answers we should like, but it does at least tend to expose the inadequate answers, thus enabling us to dismiss them from further consideration. This is, at least, a very useful contribution.

The nature of causal connections is fully explored in Schutt (1996, p.107; see the 'Further reading' section).

— Developing new policy strategies —

Arguably the prime function of research is to contribute to human knowledge, but in addition research is crucial in enabling individuals, organisations and governments to make informed decisions about policy issues. Some research is actually conducted with this particular function in mind, and can be called '**policy research**'. Such research is intended to provide the data upon which policy-makers can base their decisions. In addition, policy researchers are frequently expected to analyse their data, and to provide a series of recommendations for social action.

The first stage in policy research is often to define the main concept or issue concerned. Suppose that a manufacturing company is seeking individuals or organisations to **sponsor**, in return for advertising. There is a good deal of analysis to be done before a policy decision can be taken. The company will first need to analyse the reasons for sponsoring, and the desired characteristics of the organisation to be sponsored. These might include:

- an organisation with access to potential customers;
- an organisation whose image is congruent with that of the manufacturer;
- an organisation which would enhance the image of the product.

For example, a manufacturer of equipment for outdoor pursuits and mountaineering, might sponsor a school expedition, but it would probably wish to carry out a certain amount of market research before committing a large sum of money to it. It might wish to know about:

- the publicity that will be received by the expedition;
- the likely number of articles about the expedition in magazines and journals;
- the circulation figures of such journals;
- the number of other, similar expeditions which might thus be influenced to purchase its products.

Such market research is essential for companies who are developing a sponsorship policy. They will take a decision based upon the market data, as to whether this type of sponsorship is likely, on balance, to increase their sales figures.

Research data is also very important when colleges and universities are creating a policy on the new kinds of courses which might be developed. When formulating this type of policy it is essential to have data on, for example, the kinds of technology in current use in industry. If universities produce graduates who are in any sense out of step with the needs of industry, then they will not obtain employment, and the courses which they took will tend to lose their credibility. In order to maintain a high level of relevance, it is therefore important for universities systematically to monitor and research the needs of potential employers. Anderson and Biddle (1991; see the 'Further reading' section) contains an interesting collection of papers on the relationship between research and policy in the field of education.

Large organisations, including governments, will conduct some data gathering themselves, but will also frequently commission research from outside agencies, including universities. It is very important that the agencies which are commissioned to carry out this type of research maintain a policy of strict impartiality. It is essential that, from the very beginning of such arrangements, clear contractual terms are agreed, which set out the duties of both the sponsor and the researcher.

Policy research does not presuppose any particular methodology and, indeed, will frequently be interdisciplinary in approach. Policy-makers may wish to examine an issue from as wide a variety of viewpoints as possible before reaching a decision.

Finally, policy research may not need to be reported in quite the same way as conventional research. For one thing, the sponsors of some types of research may be more interested in a concise summary of the findings, rather than in a detailed exposition of the research methodology. Their primary focus will be the recommendations deriving from the research, and it may be that an '**executive summary**' will be more appropriate than a long, detailed report.

NEW CONCEPTS

Causal connection	Mean
Executive summary	Policy research
Macro level	Sponsor

PLANNING AN
INVESTIGATION

3

PROJECT DESIGN

—— Defining a research problem ——

When you are beginning research, the first stage is to define a topic worthy of investigation. This can be easier said than done. It is often the case that lots of possible themes come to mind, but deciding on just one of these can be difficult. One strategy is to start by thinking of a broad area which interests you. This might be, for example, local elections, computers in teaching, or management styles. These are very broad areas, and need to be defined and narrowed down much more before they become suitable for investigation.

Having decided on a broad topic, the next stage is to start collecting as much general information on it as possible. This might include newspaper cuttings, journal articles, books, tape recordings and your own notes. The purpose of this is to begin to 'map the field', and to make yourself aware of the different facets of the wider area. It is also worthwhile carrying out a literature search to identify any previous research done in the area. A rather more precise research issue should begin to surface from all of this background information. It would be much better, for example, to investigate voting patterns in local elections from 1980 to 1990 rather than simply local elections. Similarly, a study of democratic management styles in two manufacturing companies is a more focused topic than simply management styles.

A totally different way of defining a research topic is not to identify a particular issue, but to review in general the kinds of research which have been carried out in a particular area. Having identified an interesting research study, the next step is to read it, and to pose yourself the question 'Where do we go from here?' Think of possible follow-up research projects. Analyse ways in which the previous research could be supplemented, and formulate a plan designed to achieve this. In other words, build your research idea upon the work previously carried out by someone else. This is sound research practice, and many research reports and theses suggest in their conclusions, ways in which others might want to develop their research further.

It is sometimes helpful to develop a research idea in conjunction with other people. If you are part of a team of people, you might decide to research collectively a particular topic, but for each individual to take one aspect of it. Apart from the benefits of examining the broad theme from a variety of points of view, it is often very supportive to research alongside other people.

Another means of identifying a research topic is to ask an individual or an organisation if they would like you to research something for them. Many organisations would like to have issues researched, but either have neither the personnel nor the money to carry out the research. Commercial organisations, for example, are frequently interested in any data about attitudes to their products. This often helps their marketing strategy. Organisations which provide services to the public are also usually interested in receiving evaluations of those services.

Finally, another approach is to think of something which seems to need improving. Very often this might be an aspect of life where you work or are a student. For instance, you might be a student at college and feel that there should be better facilities for leaving motor cycles during the day. Before presenting your petition, you may want to carry out a survey to see if other students feel the same way.

- Take a personal interest and then narrow it down;
- build upon existing research;
- adopt a team approach;
- inquire of an individual or organisation;
- find something that may need improving.

Figure 3.1 Summary of strategies for defining a research issue

Choosing a topic to research is, however, only part of the decision-making process. There are several practical questions which it is wise to ask yourself before proceeding with the research. First of all, it is worth considering the type of data which you will need to collect. You need to be sure that you understand the data-collection strategy, and that you are familiar with any theoretical principles involved. Some background reading, or advice from your tutor, should help here.

Related to this is the question of **access**. It is sometimes quite easy to think up an interesting subject for research, but if you cannot manage to collect the necessary data then the research will not get under way. Access problems can be of various kinds. Suppose, for example, that you wanted to investigate the equal opportunities policy of an organisation. The managing director may feel that this topic should be confidential to the organisation, and that it is potentially too contentious for an outsider to research. Equally, any organisation, whether it is a school, business, or public sector service, may be sensitive about its public image, and may be reluctant to allow a researcher access to the inner areas of its working. Distance and convenience may also be relevant factors: if you pick a research topic for which the data must be collected from a long way away, or only at inconvenient times, then this may make the research impossible to carry out.

A very important issue is whether you feel that you possess the knowledge and expertise to analyse the data that you will collect. For this you need an understanding of relevant concepts, as well as the ability to arrange the data and draw the appropriate conclusions. Depending upon the approach you are taking, you may need a knowledge of statistics. Not all researchers have this kind of knowledge when they start on a project; they sometimes build up their knowledge and skills in methodology as they proceed. This is perfectly satisfactory as long as you have access to good texts and/or tutorial help. It is dangerous if you start on a project and are unaware of the exact way in which you will analyse the data; you may find that you need skills which you cannot acquire. So the basic rules are:

- be sure that you are clear about the kind of methodology which you will use;
- be sure that you either understand it now, or can definitely obtain the right kind of written or tutorial help.

A useful book for help in developing new themes for research is Porter and Coggin (1995, Chapter 2; see 'Further reading' section).

——— The importance of a design ———

The early stages of the research process involve the identification of a broad research issue, and a subsequent narrowing-down to a series of more precise aims. These aims may incorporate one or more hypotheses which are to be tested. Having achieved this degree of focus for the research, the next stage is to develop a design for the research process.

A research design incorporates answers to the following kinds of question:

- What sort of data do I need to collect in order to test the hypotheses and/or achieve the research aims?
- Where will I collect the data?
- How will I collect the data?
- What type of data-collection instrument and procedure will I use?
- Who will provide me with the data?
- Do I need to ask permission before trying to collect data?
- When will I collect the data?
- How will the data be analysed?
- Will I use a particular theoretical framework in order to interpret the data?

A research design will probably include answers to a good many other questions, but these are some of the main ones. Creswell (1994, Chapter 1) and Hakim (1987, Chapter 1) examine some of the important initial questions in developing a research design (see the 'Further reading' section).

The research design is a clearly planned procedure for carrying out the research summarised in the aims or hypotheses. The design should include all of the main features of the anticipated research, and should be capable of being understood by another researcher who is familiar with the subject area and methodology.

The selected research design is very much a function of the nature of the aims of the research. Suppose that we consider a particular research topic, such as the working lives of doctors. This is a general topic, and a specific research design will be developed depending upon the defined aims. A list of **aims** is developed in Figure 3.2 in relation to the above research issue, and in each case an example is given of the type of design which could be used to address the aims.

1 AIMS
1.1 To analyse the types of social interaction which take place in the surgery and during a home visit.
1.2 To describe and analyse the culture of the doctor–patient interaction.
COMMENT
The emphasis upon social interaction, and on the culture of a particular environment, suggests that an ETHNOGRAPHIC research design would be appropriate.

2 AIMS
2.1 To investigate whether the workloads of doctors appear to have changed over a 20-year period.
2.2 To investigate whether public attitudes to doctors have changed over this same period.
COMMENT
The focus upon the extent of change over a fairly prolonged period of time suggests that a HISTORICAL research design would be appropriate.

3 AIMS
3.1 To explore the ways in which doctors perceive requests made by patients.
3.2 To investigate the ways in which doctors weigh and balance the ethical aspects of their jobs.
COMMENT
These aims are concerned with the attitudes of doctors, and the way in which they construct their own world view. In order to collect data on this, it will probably be necessary to adopt an INTERVIEW-BASED research design.

4 AIMS
4.1 To analyse the ways in which doctors use question-and-answer techniques to help them reach a diagnosis for a patient.
4.2 To analyse the ways in which a doctor employs language and non-verbal communication in order to help patients feel relaxed.
COMMENT
These aims are concerned with data which can be gathered quite satis-factorily by observation or tape recording, and thus lend themselves to a STRUCTURED-OBSERVATION research design.

5 AIMS

5.1 To document and analyse the working life of an individual doctor.

5.2 To describe and analyse the different tasks and activities undertaken by an individual doctor.

COMMENT

As these aims involve the detailed study of a single doctor, then a CASE-STUDY design would be very appropriate.

6 AIMS

6.1 To investigate whether doctors in general feel that pressures and workloads are increasing.

6.2 To investigate whether the workloads of doctors are similar in different parts of the country.

COMMENT

As the aims are concerned with collecting data from a large number of doctors, in order to establish general trends, then a SURVEY design would be the most appropriate.

Figure 3.2 The working lives of doctors; research designs

The type of research design selected therefore depends very much upon the nature of the research aims. However, it is worth adding that these research designs are not necessarily mutually exclusive, and may be combined in a variety of ways, depending upon the research problem. Gill and Johnson (1991, Chapter 9; see the 'Further reading' section) explore the different reasons for selecting one methodology rather than another.

Having selected a research design, it is now necessary to consider the nature of the data to be collected.

——— The nature of the data ———

Different types of research design are likely to generate very different kinds of data. A survey design, for example, will often produce fairly precise, quantifiable data. An ethnographic design, or **structured-observation**, on the other hand, will tend to generate descriptive, qualitative data, at least in the first instance. The nature of the data which you, as the researcher, are collecting, can often have a variety of consequences in terms of, say, practical issues like storage and handling.

In general terms, qualitative data is much more voluminous than quantitative data. If you are conducting case-study, interview or ethnographic research, you will probably amass very large amounts of data. The following issues may then need to be considered:

- Large amounts of documentary data need a systematic filing system. It may be necessary to invest in a filing cabinet, or to improvise one with a series of cardboard compartments.
- Interview data may be in the original form of video or audio tapes, which will require careful labelling and storage. When the tapes are transcribed, they will generate numerous **transcripts**, which need to be dated, and the names of respondents noted.
- Case-study and observational research may result in notebooks, papers, documents, photographs and other items. These will require careful dating and annotation.

If qualitative data is being collected, it is worth thinking ahead as to how the data will be managed and stored. When it comes to the analysis of the data, and the writing-up of the research, it is easy to overlook important information simply because it was not easily accessed. It is important that your data-management system enables you to recall and access all of the collected data, otherwise only a partial picture will be presented.

Quantitative data, on the other hand, is generally fairly concise, although if there is a large **sample** in a survey, then this will generate a lot of questionnaires. Such data, however, usually lends itself to a process of data summary. In order to achieve this, it is essential to consider honestly whether you possess the mathematical skills necessary to analyse the data. You may need a suitable computer package to help you.

Finally, you may have decided on the kind of data that you wish to collect, and from whom you will collect it, but you may have overlooked asking potential respondents if they will co-operate. It is so easy to assume that people will be as interested and enthusiastic about a research project as you are. After all, it is your project, but there may be no obligation upon others to help. It is definitely worth making some informal inquiries at the design stage, just to set your mind at rest regarding the co-operation of respondents.

Choosing a sample

When conducting research, it is not only important to ask the question:

What are we researching?

but also to ask:

To whom does this research apply?

For example, we might plan a research design to investigate the attitudes of parents to the food which their children eat. In other words, the answer to the first question is that we are researching parental attitudes. However, parents of young children may have a different attitude to food than, say, parents of teenage children. The issues may thus be seen as being different. Parents of very young children may have almost total control over what they eat, while with teenage children there will be much less control. It is important in the research design to define the type of parents for whom the research is intended. Even if we identify parents of children under the age of two years, this will certainly be a very large group of people in the country as a whole. We may feel that it is more sensible or manageable to consider only such parents in one county, or perhaps in a single town. Once this is decided, then this large group of potential respondents becomes the 'target population', or more simply, the **'population'**.

The population is the group of people to which the research applies. When the research is finally completed, and conclusions drawn from it, then it is to these people that the researcher will apply the results. The assumption is that the research results cannot be considered to apply to those parents outside the research population.

Having established the target population within the research design, it is often the case that there are too many individuals in that population for the researcher to contact. Even if it is possible to identify the names of all the parents of children under the age of two years within a particular geographical area, it may still be very difficult in practical terms to contact them all. This situation arises frequently in research, and the solution is to select only some of the parents, on the assumption that the results received from them can be applied to the others with reasonable confidence. This smaller research group, which is considered to be typical of the target population as a whole, is called a 'sample'. Marshall and Rossman (1989, p.54; see the 'Further reading' section) provide advice on the identification of both research location and sample.

In a perfect situation, we would not need to take samples, because we would be able to collect data from every individual in the target population. As this is usually impractical, we must take a sample which is as representative of the total population as possible. When the results for the sample have been collected and analysed, the researcher will try to generalise from this data messages that are pertinent to the target population. In other words, the assumption is that whatever appears to be true for the sample is also likely to be true for the whole population.

In general, the larger the size of the sample, and the more closely the sample size approaches that of the target population, then the more confident we can be about generalising. On the other hand, the smaller the sample, then the less confident we can normally be about generalising.

————————— Collection of data —————————

One of the most important questions regarding data collection to consider is whether you can be assured of easy access to the place where you intend to carry out the research. The place where data is actually collected is often referred to as 'the field'. Research 'in the field' is often contrasted with 'desk research', or research in a laboratory. **Field research** may take place in a school or college, in an industrial organisation, or in any kind of social setting in which people can be observed. There is often no problem with gaining access to the field. If you are conducting observational research, there are many settings in which access is not a problem, in which you would be able to wander around undisturbed. Gaining access can be difficult, however, when it comes to formal organisations, which understandably do not necessarily want to admit total strangers without due reason. It can be all too easy to develop an interesting and worthwhile research design only to discover later that it is difficult to collect the data because of problems with access to the field. The causes of such difficulties may include the following:

- the research setting may be too far away, and it may be either too costly or too time-consuming (or both) to travel there to collect data;
- it may be difficult to obtain permission to obtain access to the field;
- even if access is gained relatively easily, the social dynamics of the situation may make it difficult to relate to all the respondents as hoped.

With regard to the first point, it is quite easy to think of interesting research issues in exciting locations, but making sure that you are able to get there is a very different matter. Research often entails making regular visits to the field to collect data, and even a fairly short round trip can prove expensive when made frequently over a regular, prolonged period. This is not to say that you should not be ambitious in your research, but rather that you should be circumspect from the beginning about the scale of your commitment.

Another matter to consider regarding the collection of data is whether it is appropriate to use others to help you with the task, or indeed to work as part of a research team. It is accepted practice in some research designs to use associates or assistants to help collect the data. This is particularly the case in survey research. Many of us will have been stopped on the high street by people working for marketing or research organisations who want to ask us our opinions. Government statistical information about the family, education and employment patterns is sometimes collected by research assistants by means of telephone surveys. In universities it is also a fairly common practice for a professor or other senior member of staff to direct a research project, while a group of supervised research students collect a good deal of the data, and assist with the analysis. By taking part in this way, the students advance their knowledge of research methodology, and learn something about the organisation and management of a large-scale research project.

Whenever this type of approach is used, however, there are a number of potential problem areas which should be considered in advance:

- if a number of different people are conducting interviews with **respondents**, then they may ask questions in slightly different ways, which could undermine the trustworthiness of the data. Attempts should be made to standardise the presentation of the questions as much as possible;

- the sampling strategy should be determined very carefully and precisely by the person planning the research, and this policy should be carried out in as standardised a way as possible by the research assistants. Ideally, those collecting the data should not be called upon to take any sampling decisions. If sampling decisions are devolved to a number of individuals, this increases the risk of inconsistencies in the research;
- regular meetings of the researchers should be held in order to develop a team philosophy, and to minimise the danger of people developing too individualistic an approach to the data collection.

Nevertheless, the idea of a team approach to research is very popular. It can be interesting to work with others on a shared project, and it is possible to collect much more comprehensive data in a shorter time.

Data analysis

It is easy to get the impression that research does (or should) proceed in a step-by-step, sequential fashion. The assumption can be made that research starts with a review of the literature, continues with data collection followed by data analysis, and concludes with the writing of the research report. Although this is perfectly accurate as a summary of the research process, it does not really reflect the complexity of the activity. Research is probably more realistically seen as a series of overlapping activities, or even as a network of activities which often proceed simultaneously.

This view applies very much to the processes of data collection and analysis. It is very difficult, for example, to resist the temptation to analyse the data a little as it is collected. In fact, it can be argued that this is at times a much more productive process than waiting until all the data has been assembled. Much depends upon the research design. In a very precisely structured experimental design, it may be more appropriate to collect all the data before attempting to analyse it. However, in ethnographic and case-study research, for example, it can often be very useful to analyse the data as it is collected.

The reason for this is that each stage of analysis can suggest a slightly different approach to sampling, or to the type of data collected. To some extent, such research can proceed in unanticipated directions, with each stage contributing to the solution of the overall research problem.

This approach to data analysis starts with the development of a research issue, or perhaps some fairly precise hypotheses. A general research design is developed and some initial data collected. The data is then analysed, particularly with a view to arranging it systematically and checking whether there are any underlying concepts inherent in the data. Supposing that respondents are using several different key ideas in the data, it may then be decided to explore only some of these. Perhaps the data-collection instrument is amended to reflect this decision at this stage. More data is then collected and subjected to the same kind of analysis. There may then be a refocusing upon only part of the data. This kind of process continues until the researcher is satisfied with the exploration of the original research issue.

Sometimes this type of data analysis is very helpful in detecting flaws in the design of the research. In a hypothetical case, consider an **action-research** project to investigate the effects on staff in a large company or organisation of having a stress counsellor available for two hours per week. It transpires that very little data can be collected because so few staff attend the sessions. However, independent research suggests that a considerable number of staff experience stress at work. Evidence from the one or two who attend suggests that people are not going to the counselling room because they are too embarrassed to make an appointment. This initial data analysis can then be used to reorganise the provision of counselling, and subsequently to restructure the research programme. This approach to research design, and to the **analysis of data**, suggests a much more integrative model of research, in which all of the constituent elements combine to help resolve an issue.

The process of data analysis is understandably very complex, and varies according to the particular research design and methodology which is used. However, all types of analysis have some basic features in common, and it worth looking briefly at some of these. Some purposes of analysis are set out in Figure 3.3.

To summarise
Most researchers collect more data than they can easily use in their final reports. One of the early stages of analysis involves trying to reduce that mass of information into a more easily managed form. It is sometimes difficult to proceed with the analysis until this has been done.

To categorise
The process of summarising often involves dividing up the data into sections. These divisions are often not 'naturally occurring' in the data, and the researcher has to decide which ideas or concepts can usefully form the basis for categories.

To develop linkages
The next stage of analysis is very often to look for apparent linkages and connections between the categories. These connections might take the form of hypothetical causal connections which will need much more specific investigation. When the analysis has reached the stage of proposing possible connections between categories, it is often the case that further data collection and analysis is required in order to establish the status of such connections.

Explanation
The process of establishing connections between variables almost inevitably leads to questions about explanation. We want to know why variables are connected and whether one variable influences another directly. When we are slowly able to resolve some of these questions, we are at the stage of developing a theory. This is a general statement which links together a number of variables in an overall explanation of a phenomenon.

Prediction
The development of a theory, however tentative, paves the way to being able to estimate how phenomena will react in the future. If we can begin to understand and explain the way in which variables interact now, then we should be able to anticipate to some extent their interaction in new situations.

To propose new hypotheses
The development of a theory which appears to be reasonably good at explanation and prediction is not the end of the analytical process. Such a theory will almost certainly suggest relationships between variables which should exist if the theory is viable. These hypothetical statements derive directly from the theory.

Test hypotheses

These hypotheses must then be tested to see if they can be verified, and hence that the theory can be supported. More empirical data is thus collected, and used to either support or to negate the hypothesis. In the case of the negation of the hypothesis, it may be necessary to revise the theory to some extent. In principle, this process of developing a theory and then subjecting it to a testing procedure can go on until no contrary cases can be found. The theory can then be given provisional support.

Figure 3.3 The purposes of analysis

Many research projects will not include all of the stages of analysis shown in Figure 3.3. Much depends upon the scale of the research, and on the degree of sophistication which is desired. Nevertheless, these are some of the important elements of analysis.

When collecting data, it is useful to remember that eventually it will have to be analysed. It is worth thinking carefully about the quantity of data which will be required, as some techniques generate a very large amount of information. Taped interviews are a case in point.

It is also not the norm to present large quantities of raw data in a research report, either in the text or in the appendix. If the data is quantitative, then much of it should be reduced to a tabular or statistical form, while with qualitative data it is often possible to use only certain extracts from the data which have particular significance for the research.

Generalisation

Once the process of data analysis is complete, one of the main aims of a research project is to be able to say with some degree of confidence that the results apply to a wider population. Perhaps the most desirable situation is for a researcher to be able to develop a theory which is so general in its relevance that it is universally applicable. However, it is seldom possible to do this. Most research has much more limited applicability because of the variety of factors which influence the research process and its outcomes.

One of the most important of these factors is that the actual process of research can affect the respondent. Sometimes simply asking a person to think about an issue during an interview, for example, can cause them to develop a wider perception than is typical of the population at large. We might give someone a questionnaire on the subject of euthanasia which, by the sequence of questions, causes respondents to think very carefully about the matter. It is quite possible that they will hence develop a much greater awareness of euthanasia than is typical of the general population. Moreover, respondents may also be motivated to visit a library and read around the subject.

The general result is that long-term changes in knowledge and attitudes may be brought about within the research sample. These changes will render this group substantially different from the population, and will make generalisation much more difficult. Effects which are the result of the experimental procedure are termed reactive effects.

NEW CONCEPTS

Access	Population
Action research	Respondent
Aims	Sample
Analysis of data	Structured observation
Field research	Transcript

4

BASIC RESEARCH CONCEPTS

Research is a systematic, planned activity, and there is reasonable consensus over the types of procedures which are acceptable. There is also fairly common agreement over the central concepts which are essential in research. It is therefore worth being familiar with such terms, and their use in research discussions. We have mentioned some concepts, such as 'sampling', already. This chapter is devoted to explaining a number of these basic and important ideas.

———— Sampling strategies ————

In the previous chapter, we discussed some general principles about sampling, and mentioned the significance of sample size when it comes to generalising to a wider population. However, it is not simply the size of the sample which affects our confidence about generalising; it is also very important how the sample is selected. The most representative type of sample would be one in which every individual person in the target population had an equal chance of being selected for the sample. On the other hand, if we simply chose people whom we happened to meet on a particular day, then this type of sample would not be likely to be very representative. A great deal depends upon the sampling procedures.

We can distinguish two main types of sample used in social science research:

- **Probability sample**;
- **Non-probability sample**.

A probability sample is one in which every member of the target population has a known chance of being selected. People are selected according to certain predetermined systems of probability. On the other hand, in a non-probability sample people are selected according to much more subjective criteria, such as whether the researcher judges them to have a suitable background or experience for the research project. These two broad approaches to sampling serve very different purposes and types of research design. There are also a number of distinctive approaches to sampling which can be grouped under each heading.

Probability samples

A simple, **random sample** is the commonest type of probability sample. It is a sample in which every member of the target population has an equal chance of being selected. The traditional way of selecting a random sample is 'to put all the names in a hat', and to select the number required. Various mechanical means of ensuring a thorough mixing of the names and numbers have also been developed.

Another method is to use tables of random numbers which have been generated by computer. In this procedure, all members of the target population are allocated a number in sequence. The researcher selects any point on the random-number tables at which to start, and then reads off the numbers in a line, moving in any direction. The members of the target population which correspond to these random numbers are then selected.

A third method is to list all the members of the target population according to a criterion which is independent of the research, such as by alphabetical order of surname. The researcher then selects individuals at known intervals down the list, such as every fifth or every tenth person. This is known as a **systematic sample**, and is a very easy means of selecting a random sample, but has one main difficulty: lists can sometimes contain trends which are difficult to identify, and which create a non-random sample. A common example is that in an employer's staff list the most senior members of staff may precede the others. Also, in an alphabetical list, if two people have the same surname, then even if one is selected the other has no chance of selection. The sample cannot therefore be a truly random sample, since not everyone has an equal chance of selection.

Another problematic issue with the 'drawing out of the hat' approach is that, strictly-speaking, each name or number should be replaced in the hat once it has been selected and noted. This ensures that the sample is selected from the total population on each occasion on which a name is drawn. If the same name is drawn on a second occasion, then it is simply replaced and the selection repeated.

A variant of random sampling can be used in which the target population consists of a number of clearly defined groups which are of interest to the researcher. For example, consider a study in which ethnic origin is one of the important factors. If a simple random sample is taken of a mixed-ethnic population, then some of the ethnic groups may not be represented in the final sample. This kind of situation happens by chance in random sampling, and in this case may be counterproductive to the research. The problem can be avoided by considering each ethnic subgroup of the population as being a separate entity, and drawing a simple random sample from each subgroup. Each subgroup can be considered as a section or stratum of the overall population, and hence this sampling procedure is termed a **stratified random sample**. The strata will typically each be of different size, and it is often the case that the researcher will draw a sample which is proportionate to the size of each stratum.

It is much better to define the strata in terms of a criterion important to the research design. For example, the educational background of respondents can be used as the basis for strata, but only if education is an important variable in the research.

A final type of probability sample in common use is the cluster sample. This is used particularly when data is being gathered from large geographical areas. Suppose, for instance, that it is necessary to survey the residents of an inner-city area. There may be no adequate listing of these residents, and the population may be very large. The approach of cluster sampling is to divide up the area into a number of sections, and then to take a random sample of these sections. The sections may be obtained by drawing a series of grid lines across a map of the area, or by dividing it up into groups of streets of roughly equal size. The next step is to divide each group of streets or lesser area into smaller sections, perhaps each comprising a group of houses or blocks of flats. A random sample is then taken of these. Finally, a random sample is taken from each group of houses, resulting ultimately in a list of individual residents who will act as respondents. It can thus be seen that cluster sampling is a multistage process, which enables the researcher to cope with sampling within a large, dispersed population.

Let us now turn to samples which have no statistical probability significance.

Non-probability samples

These are also sometimes known as 'purposive' samples. Perhaps the most obvious example is what we might call a fortuitous, or convenience, sample. This is when we utilise whatever instance or example is available to us. If we were to try to conduct a survey by simply stopping people on the street who were willing to talk to us, then this may be convenient, but it would scarcely be a sample in any meaningful sense of the word. However, some researchers have to utilise those objects which happen to be available, and cannot afford the luxury of choosing a probability sample. Palaeontologists, for example, are often delighted to analyse any fossil that they can find, rather than waiting until they can take a representative sample. They must work under the assumption that the few instances of a particular fossilised animal in existence are actually typical of other, previously existing members of the species.

A commonly used type of purposive sampling is key-informant sampling. A **key informant** is someone who has a specialist, insider knowledge of the research issue, and is therefore able to supply the kind of data which it is unlikely that others would be able to provide. A researcher may use one or more key informants in a study. A sample may be composed of one or two key informants, as well as a range of others who are less well informed.

The researcher may identify key informants in a variety of ways. Firstly, they may hear about the research and offer their services in providing data. Secondly, others may name them as being likely sources of valuable information; and finally, they may be selected by the researcher as a result of preliminary data collection or observation. When a person offers help with a research project on the grounds that they possess special information, it is perhaps worthwhile being cautious, just in case the data provided is biased in some way. It is always important to check for bias by contrasting what has been said with the comments obtained from other key informants.

A variant of key-informant sampling is the **snowball sample**, when initial contacts or key informants are asked to name other people who may have specialist knowledge. When these people have provided data, they are asked for the names of others who may be willing to help, and so on. The purpose is to establish a chain of 'expert witnesses'. The value of such informants depends very much upon the kind of description given to the nominating respondent. It is important to describe very clearly the qualities, knowledge, employment status and other characteristics required in a potential respondent. Only then can we expect a nominee to be in the correct category for the research.

Snowball sampling may raise ethical questions, particularly as to whether nominees should be told the name of the person who has nominated them. It is worthwhile thinking out the procedures clearly before the research begins, as some people may object to having been named as potential informants.

A discussion of approaches to sampling is contained in Black (1993, Chapter 3; see the 'Further reading' section).

—— Multiple method approaches ——

One of the main characteristics of research problems is that they tend to be very complex. It is often the case that they cannot even be partially resolved by using a single approach. Suppose that the personnel officer for a large company is asked to review the procedures relating to the interviewing and appointment of staff, and as part of the review to research the attitudes of existing employees to the process by which they were appointed. Such a research task could turn out to be very complex indeed. Employees of the company may at first well feel reluctant to talk about their experiences during recruitment, in case they said something which affected their future prospects in the company. The researcher could certainly not be sure that respondents were giving their real feelings or true opinions.

It may therefore help to employ a variety of data-collection techniques in order to explore different aspects of the research issue. A questionnaire could be used to collect data concerning the extent to which everyone received the same documentation during the recruitment process. Informal interviews could help to reveal some of the attitudes towards the process. Documents in personnel files could be used to shed light on some aspects of the recruitment process, and particularly on differences in the treatment of individuals.

The key question which should be asked by a researcher when choosing a methodology is:

What is the appropriate method or methods to resolve this question?

The nature of the research problem should drive the choice of methodology. The researcher should be trying to assemble the best set of methodological devices to resolve the research question. There is often a tendency to use the same methodology for different research issues without thinking critically about whether it is appropriate.

The other important aspect about the choice of methodology is that the very act of choosing predetermines, to some extent, the type of data to be collected, and the kind of conclusions which will be drawn. A particular methodology can in a sense be seen as a unique strategy for examining a problem, and will provide only restricted insights. It could be argued that the choice by a researcher of a specific method is fundamentally ideological in nature, reflecting the perspective of the researcher, and giving a distinctive picture of the issue.

It is important that we bear in mind the range of methods available, and choose the one (or ones) which seem best suited to the problem, irrespective of our own preferences. This philosophy is at the heart of the multiple method approach.

Triangulation

The use of multiple methods is very much linked to the concept of **triangulation**. In research, and particularly in social-science research, the phenomena we are investigating are very complex, in the sense of including a large number of variables. Much social-science research involves some aspect of individual or group human behaviour, and the latter is often very difficult either to understand or to predict. When we are not clear why someone is behaving in a certain way, we often ask other people for their opinion. By collecting a range of opinions, we are sometimes more able to build up our own picture of behavioural patterns.

When there has been an accident at the workplace, the investigator may ask witnesses individually to provide an account of the circumstances. The accounts may all differ to some extent, but a synthesis of them should provide an account which is as near to the actual event as possible. We might call this observational triangulation.

The word 'triangulation' is taken from the use of bearings when trying to locate a position on a map. If we know the bearing of point A from point B, we know the direction of A, but not how far away from B it is. If, however, we also know the bearing of point A from point C, then we know that A lies where the two bearings intersect. The idea of using bearings from two known positions to define the location of a third gives us the term 'triangulation'.

In science, however, triangulation does not necessarily mean using only two observers to try to understand an event. The researcher will typically employ as many observers, and as many different types of data, as can reasonably be used for the purposes of the research. Just as there are advantages to this approach, there are also disadvantages. The very advantages of having multiple perspectives and viewpoints go hand in hand with the drawbacks caused by the different data-collection techniques used by individuals. As part of an interview survey, for example, several different interviewers may all use the same standard interview schedule. There will, however, probably be differences in the way in which the questions are asked. Even assuming that all the interviewers read out the same questions exactly as they are printed, there will still be differences in tone of voice and facial expression. These differences in presentation can, of course, cause significant differences in the nature of the data provided, and should be considered in the analysis.

Triangulation can also involve the collection of several sets of data using the same methodology. This often takes the form of the repetition of a research project in order to check whether the data and results are consistent. This is an important type of methodological triangulation, and is sometimes known as 'within methods' triangulation.

The use of different methods to focus on the same research issue remains a very important research technique. One of the many advantages with such 'between methods' triangulation is that one method may complement another. For example, when researchers devise a questionnaire, they are inevitably constructing questions which they see as being significant. These questions may not, however, be the ones which are significant to the respondents. To help with this situation, informal, open-ended interviews conducted prior to the questionnaire being written can provide very useful background data to help with producing questions which are significant for both respondent and researcher. Triangulation in one form or another is thus a very important aspect of a good research design. A review of the issue of triangulation is available in Bryman (1988, p.131; see the 'Further reading' section).

Reliability

When we have collected data as part of a research investigation, we would like to think that if the research was repeated at some time in the future the results would be identical. We might imagine the situation in a chemistry laboratory where we are measuring the melting point of a solid. If we take a sample from the same jar of chemical each time we carry out the test, we might assume that the readings would be identical. We might then ask a colleague to carry out some measurements, and again we would probably assume that the temperature reading would be almost the same. It is true that it is a reasonable assumption that the readings would be close but, in fact, when measurements such as these are taken some time apart, they can be affected in a number of ways. For example, in each subsequent test:

- the test tubes may be slightly different;
- a different thermometer may be used;
- the chemical may not be uniformly mixed in the storage jar, and may not yield identical samples;
- there may be impurities in the test tubes, or on the spatula;
- the thermometer may be read in a different way each time, particularly when there is a different observer.

This list could potentially be extended further: we might think about changes in air pressure and humidity between the tests, or of air impurities getting into the test tube. When we think of the problem in these terms, it is clear that absolute consistency or **reliability** of results is going to be very difficult, if not impossible, to achieve.

Moreover, the above example is taken from a physical-sciences laboratory. If it is difficult to achieve reliability in such a context, it is probably going to be even harder in a social-science context, with human beings as research subjects. With humans as subjects it is much more difficult to know if the qualities or attributes which we are measuring have remained constant. The opinions which individuals hold, for example, frequently change with time. We often change our opinion about issues, depending upon what we hear on the radio or television, or read in the newspapers. Data collected about people's opinions will probably show relatively low reliability, but it will be difficult to be sure whether this is a reflection of the changing of opinion, or of lack of reliability in the measurement process.

In the human sciences, many forms of data collection are inherently unreliable, particularly when they are used by different researchers. Observational data is an obvious case in point. Different researchers will almost inevitably concentrate upon distinct aspects of whatever is being observed. They will give a different emphasis to their observations, and this will be reflected in their research notes. This effect is even likely to be present if they are given a fairly precisely written observational schedule. This may reduce the observer effect, but as individuals we all observe phenomena from a slightly different viewpoint.

Interview data also tends to have a low level of reliability because of the almost inevitable influence of the interviewer upon the inter-action with the interviewee. In a very formal, structured interview the interviewer effects may be reduced, but in an informal interview, in which there is little predictable structure to the event, then there will tend to be much lower reliability.

Finally, as an example of a data-collection technique of relatively high reliability, we might consider the postal questionnaire. This minim-ises the intrusion of the researcher, but reliability depends very much upon the nature of the questions. Highly structured, closed questions may tend to have a higher reliability than open-ended questions which ask the respondent to write a paragraph in response.

The most straightforward method for judging reliability is to use a data-collection instrument on two separate occasions, and to measure the degree of consistency between the two sets of results. This is often known as 'test-retest' reliability. The significant factor here may be the time interval between the test and retest. If this is short, the respondent's memory of the first test may well affect their perform-ance on the second test. On the other hand, if the time interval is lengthened, there may be actual changes in the respondent's opinions, which are caused by normal development over time. The retest results would be substantially different, but this would not be due to any inherent lack of reliability in the measuring instrument. Considerable thought therefore needs to be given to this time interval.

A different strategy of trying to assess reliability is to devise two different forms of measuring instrument in order to minimise learning effects on the part of respondents. In other words, performance in the first test would probably have a minimal influence on performance in the retest. This should give a useful measure of reliability, providing only that there is a high reliability between the two versions of the data-collection instrument.

We can now consider a concept which is intimately connected with reliability, and that is **validity**.

Validity

Let us suppose that we are conducting research into the staff-appraisal system of a large organisation. We devise an interview schedule for staff respondents, and one of the questions which we ask is:

Do you consider that the staff-appraisal system is fairly administered?

If the respondents answer 'yes' to this question, then we may suppose that they believe the appraisal system to be organised and run in an equitable manner. Now, if the respondents actually do believe this (as opposed, for example, to simply saying what they think the researcher might want them to say), and have answered the question honestly, then we can say that the research is valid. In other words, research is valid if it measures what the researcher intends it to measure.

In the above example, however, it may be that the respondents are unwilling to say exactly what they believe. Perhaps they think that the appraisal system is really very unfair, but feel that it may prejudice future appraisals if they go on record as saying this to an interviewer. They therefore decide not to reveal their true feelings in the interview. The research would thus not be valid. If, however, the same question is asked in an anonymous, postal questionnaire, the respondents may feel that there is no harm in writing exactly what they believe, because their identities cannot be disclosed. In this situation, the research will be valid. The research has measured what it was intended to measure.

We might therefore well judge that the methods used to collect data can make a difference to the findings. If this is so for a particular investigation, then the first set of data must have low validity, because another way of trying to measure the same phenomenon gives different results. We cannot be sure that the first measurement was actually measuring what was intended.

Research of high validity occurs when we measure a phenomenon in a variety of ways, and obtain the same results independently of the methods. This signifies that it is likely that we have collected data on the actual issue which we wanted to investigate.

Part of the difficulty of estimating the validity of some research results is that when we come to remeasure the factor concerned it may well have changed. This is particularly so when measuring human qualities and characteristics. We are probably well aware of the developmental nature of many human characteristics. Human beings grow psychologically as they face and overcome new challenges, and may change their attitudes and beliefs with time. It is thus very difficult to know that we are measuring the identical entity on two different occasions, and it is thus hard to be certain that the results of the first measurement were valid.

A closely related problem is that of changes in the environment since the first measurement was taken. Suppose we are measuring aspects of people's political views. During the space of time from the first measurement to the second, the respondents will have been subject to many political events that have been reported in the media, and we cannot be at all sure that they will not have changed their political views as a result. We cannot eliminate some environmental changes, and they make an estimate of validity very difficult indeed.

A further issue with validity checks is that the researcher too may actually have changed by the time that the second validity check is made. When you are conducting a series of interviews, it is almost certain that you will change your approach during the research. There is no guarantee that the researcher is asking questions in a consistent manner, and hence it is not easy to confirm validity.

The means of gathering data can also make validity checks difficult. However, the crucial factor here is whether the data-collection process is part of the normal experience of the respondent. If it is, then there are likely to be fewer effects caused by the actual process of data collection. For example, if actors are the subject of the research, and we are videotaping them during rehearsals, then because they are fairly familiar with such procedures there are less likely to be any effects caused by the research procedure.

Variables

Research is very much the study of variables, and how these affect each other. We use the idea a great deal in research, and the purpose of this section is to think a little more clearly about the idea.

Perhaps we could consider an example such as industrial productivity. This idea is composed of two separate concepts, i.e. 'industry' and 'productivity'. In an everyday sense we have an understanding of what is meant by 'industry', and what is meant by 'productivity'. However, as with all concepts, we may not entirely agree about the definitions of these concepts, or on the way in which they should be used.

Suppose that we consider the case of a large engineering works manufacturing steel components. We may all agree that this comes within the definition of the concept 'industry'. However, this concept is also used much more widely these days to include such terms as the 'insurance industry', or the 'banking industry'. No one can dispute the fact that these terms are used, and therefore by usage that they must come within the concept of 'industry'. Not everyone, though, may support that use of the word 'industry'. Some people may even wish to extend the use of the term to say the 'social-work industry' or the 'caring industry'; others may disagree with this usage.

'Industry', then, is a concept. It is a practical, empirical classification of certain types of organisation or activity. It must be acknowledged, however, that individuals' views may differ regarding what should be included in that classification. What we can say, however, about industry as a concept is that we do not think of it varying by extent in the same way that we think of productivity varying. We know that productivity goes up and down depending on a variety of economic factors, and it is often artificially controlled by a company in order to meet the market conditions.

We can therefore say that industrial productivity is a variable, whereas industry is a non-variable. The concept 'industry' is simply a name for a particular phenomenon. We may not all wish to include the same examples under the umbrella term 'industry', but within a particular type of definition 'industry' as an idea is non-variable.

Industrial productivity, on the other hand, is very much a variable. We can speak of high productivity and low productivity, and of any level of productivity in between. We also know that there are many factors which can affect productivity. These might include:

- the type of technology in which a company has invested;
- the availability of raw materials;
- the policy of the company (which may be affected by such macro-economic factors as the state of the market and exchange rates).

Industrial productivity is thus a variable, the magnitude of which may well depend upon other factors.

This idea of a variable being dependent is an important concept in research. A dependent variable is one which changes when other variables change. A dependent variable may sometimes be changed by only one other variable; on the other hand, it may be affected by a complex range of variables.

The most straightforward examples of dependent variables are often to be found in physics. In a simple experiment to investigate the timing of the swing of a pendulum, it can be shown that this alters when we change the length of the pendulum. The timing of the swing thus depends upon the length of the pendulum. The timing of the swing is the dependent variable, and we term the length the independent variable. Expressing this in a different way, the independent variable is the element which we alter in order to investigate the effect upon the dependent variable. Human psychology and society is, however, often rather more complex in terms of variables than physics.

Consider the financial income of an individual. This is certainly a variable. We can think of individuals with a very wide range of incomes. If, however, we try to make conjectures about the factors which might affect income, we probably do not simply think of one variable, but of many. We might start, for example, by considering the variable of the educational level. We can probably think of people with high educational attainments who are earning a great deal. We can then think of people of relatively low educational attainment who earn the opposite. In this discussion, financial income is the dependent variable because it appears to depend upon educational attainment, which is hence the independent variable. However, just when we think that we have defined a relationship between two variables, we remember those people who have a relatively low educational attainment and who have yet earned considerable fortunes – perhaps by founding a successful business. The connection between the two variables is thus obviously not one of cause and effect. We can perhaps reflect upon other possible independent variables which might affect financial income:

- occupation of parents;
- extent of personal motivation to be wealthy;
- level of communication skills;
- career choice;
- extent of financial support from parents.

The variables affecting financial income are likely to be numerous, and to be interconnected by a complex web of relationships. Experience suggests that there is unlikely to be a straightforward, direct connection between two variables.

It is important to realise, however, that a variable is not always 'dependent' or 'independent' in all situations. In the above example, financial income is the dependent variable being studied, while educational level is the independent variable. But, the study could in a sense be reversed, and an investigation carried out of educational level as the dependent variable. We might be interested for example, in the extent to which the educational level reached by children depended upon the financial income of their parents and thus the educational opportunities which they could provide.

This discussion of the relationships between variables leads us on to the final concept in this chapter, which is **correlation**.

Correlation

A large part of research activity is concerned with trying to establish connections between variables. When we are conducting research, we often suspect that two variables are connected in some way, because when the value of one changes the value of the other seems to change as well. If two variables are changing together in some kind of systematic pattern, then we can say that they appear to show 'covariation', or that there appears to be a 'correlation' between them.

Just because there is a correlation between two variables does not mean to say that one variable causes a change in the other variable. Both variables may, in fact, be affected by a third, and as yet unidentified, variable. It is always best to be very cautious before assuming that because two variables are correlated this automatically indicates cause and effect.

Sometimes two variables are correlated so that as one increases then the other increases too, although perhaps by a different amount. On the other hand, an increase in one variable can sometimes be associated with a decrease in another. In business there may be a correlation between, say, the amount of money spent on advertising and marketing, and the sales figures for a product. The higher the advertising budget, the greater the sales. This is unlikely to be a very precise relationship because many other factors can affect the sales of products. Although an increase in one variable may generally result in an increase in the other, it may be difficult to predict the exact change.

Many relationships between variables are of this type, in which both variables increase together. However, let us consider the variables of depth of insulation in a house, and the rate of heat loss. As we provide greater depth of insulation, the rate of heat loss decreases. This is an example of an increase in one variable causing a decrease in the other.

NEW CONCEPTS

Correlation	Reliability
Key informant	Snowball sample
Multiple methods	Stratified random sample
Non-probability sample	Systematic sample
Probability sample	Triangulation
Random sample	Validity

5

ETHICAL ISSUES

———— Values and research ————

Any activity which involves interaction between human beings can raise questions regarding how we ought to behave towards each other. If we are sensitive to ethical issues, we are continually asking ourselves such questions as:

- Have I been considerate enough?
- Did I take their views into account?
- Have I been more concerned with myself than with others?

These kinds of ethical question are relevant to a research situation, particularly when data is being collected directly from human respondents. The way in which we respond to **ethics** depends very much upon our own value position in terms of relationships with others.

Ethical issues arise in research because of the complex web of rights and responsibilities which link participants together. Responsibilities can be of various types:

- the researcher has a responsibility to him- or herself to conduct research safely and sensibly;
- there is a responsibility to all respondents to make sure that they understand what they are taking part in, and how any data will be used;
- there is a responsibility to any organisations involved in the research. They should be fully informed of the nature of the research, and of any relevant implications, before they give permission for the research to go ahead;

— **61** —

- the researcher has a responsibility to her or his employer, educational institution, and to the general community of scholars, to conduct the research according to accepted conventions.

The problem with these responsibilities is that it is difficult at times to be absolutely clear as to the meaning of such terms as 'accepted conventions'. Sometimes a researcher has to make a choice about how to organise a research project, and this decision depends very much upon his or her value position. For example, the ideal conditions may not be available in which to interview people, but the researcher may decide that it is important to proceed with the research and obtain the results nevertheless. This is a value judgement. Research often involves a series of value judgements such as this.

There are rarely, if ever, clear cut-and-dried decisions where ethical issues are concerned. The best we can usually do is to analyse the issue carefully, and to try to come to the fairest and most balanced decision that we can. It is also a good idea to be willing to discuss in public the reasons for arriving at a particular decision. If we feel happy to do this, then we usually are fairly confident about the way in which we have arrived at our value judgement. Let us look now at some rather more specific issues of ethics and research.

Rights of individuals and organisations

To some extent, research always intrudes into the privacy of both individuals and organisations, and this is the source of many of the ethical dilemmas which face researchers. Just because we might have a strong desire to pursue a research study does not mean that anyone else has an obligation to help us. We might feel that the research is crucially important, and that it will be of great benefit to humanity, but others may beg to differ. Even if people agree with the importance of the research, they may equally consider that there are negative consequences for them in participating in it, and that these are more significant to them than the generally positive outcomes of the research. Potential respondents are likely to balance the perceived value of the research with its personal effects on them.

Organisations are in a similar position. Business organisations in particular are in competition with other organisations, and may not want researchers intruding into aspects of their manufacturing and marketing operations. If asked to take part in research they will, perhaps understandably, think carefully about any possible effects upon their productivity and profits.

Once researchers look at the situation from the respondent's point of view, then it is clear that it is only fair to be very careful about asking for access. We should not presume that we can automatically collect data. It is important to make a clear, and perhaps formal, request to collect data from either an individual or an organisation.

In some ways, the most considerate way in which to approach an individual or organisation is in writing. The researcher can summarise the research project and explain very clearly what is involved. The respondent, on the other hand, can take time to consider the request. Respondents are not being pressurised in any way, and can, in fact, request further information if required. Organisations usually prefer this approach, because it gives colleagues time to hold discussions with each other, and to decide whether or not the organisation wishes to proceed with the request. From the researcher's point of view, it is also not easy to know to whom the request for help should be sent in an organisation. Sending a written request provides time for the letter to be passed on to the most appropriate person.

Another very important right for both individuals and organisations is the right to withdraw from the research project. People may agree to take part at the beginning, feeling that it is an interesting research project, but they may gradually develop reservations about it. It is important that both individuals and organisations feel that they can withdraw if the research becomes unacceptable to them for any reason. It is probably easier for organisations to withdraw than for individuals; sometimes people begin to feel obliged to continue as respondents, even though they are having misgivings. As researchers, it is important not to put people under any form of stress or embarrassment during the data-collection process. It can be that an interviewee begins to find the interview process not as relaxing or pleasant as they originally thought, and yet the researcher may be unaware of this change of feeling. It is vital that the respondents feel that they can either voice their concerns and that the researcher will adapt the approach, or that they can unilaterally withdraw from the research project.

As a researcher, you will have an understandable primary concern with collecting your data and producing your results. However, in order to do this you will nearly always require the help of other people. Research is, after all, a very collaborative form of human activity. It is important from an ethical point of view to try to place yourself in the position of the respondents, and attempt to understand their position. We will now look more closely at several important ethical issues.

Informed consent

From time to time we hear of cases in which individuals have been persuaded to take part in research, and have then suffered side effects. The apparently worst cases of this seem to have involved research of a medical or military nature. Fortunately such events are relatively rare, and are minimised by the formal and informal checks which are generally in place. Whenever such situations occur, it is usually because a very important ethical principle has been breached. This is the principle of **informed consent**.

We are all autonomous human beings, and have the free will to examine a situation and to decide whether or not we wish to participate in it. However, in order to exercise our free will, we need to understand the nature of the situation, and to have a complete picture of what is going on. Only then are we truly in a position to agree to take part. In other words, we should be fully 'informed' before deciding whether or not we shall give our consent to take part.

Research is a very complex activity, and there are many aspects about which a potential participant might wish to be informed. Some of them are as follows:

- how the research project arose;
- the names of the researchers involved;
- the employers of the researchers;
- the financial sponsors of the research (if any);
- the agency or organisation which is supporting the research;
- the aims of the research;
- the nature of the data being collected;
- arrangements for publishing the results;
- whether results will be used to make policy decisions.

This is not a complete list, and there are certainly other areas which might be of interest to potential respondents in research. It is impossible and impracticable to make every detail of a research project available, and a reasonable selection of information must be made. It is a good idea to prepare a brief outline of the research which can be read in a minute or two. This can then be photocopied and given to every person who is asked to take part in the research programme. An advantage of this approach is that you can be certain that everyone receives the same information about the research, and that there have been no misunderstandings because of an omission of something.

Just as many employers organise an induction programme for new employees, it is helpful to think in terms of an induction course for your research respondents. You might wish to describe how the idea for the research arose, and what benefits should accrue from the project.

Your respondents may also be very interested in the origins of any financial support for the research, and of sponsorship. For many people, research is simply an individual activity carried out for personal rewards. In some cases, however, research is sponsored by commercial organisations, or by universities. In situations in which your respondents come from an organisation or business which might consider itself a business competitor of your sponsor, then it is probably only fair to disclose the sponsor's identity. There may be no conflict here, but respondents could be very cautious about revealing such things as marketing data. This issue leads us on to that of non-disclosure of identity.

Anonymity

Both individuals and organisations have a right to privacy. This may be both a civil or moral right, and also a legal right. For example, some organisations include in their contracts of employment a clause preventing employees from speaking publicly about the organisation. They prefer, perhaps understandably, to regulate their public pronouncements through a public-relations or media-relations officer. Acting as a research respondent may breach this obligation, and the person would probably be wise to seek the permission of their line manager.

A way in which to evade this general difficulty of securing **respondent anonymity** is to ensure that the data you collect is not attributed to a named individual or organisation and, indeed, that no clues are given which could enable anyone easily to identify the source of the information. In the case of an organisation you could invent a fictional name which gives no clues as to the organisation's real identity. It would defeat the purpose to refer to a major chocolate manufacturer as 'Chocbar Ltd', which might have the consequence of narrowing down the organisation's identity to one of only a few companies. It is much better to think of a name unassociated with the product – unless the nature of the product is significant for the research report.

Another mistake which can easily be made is to assume that one is hiding the identity of a person by describing them as, say, the head of personnel with a large car manufacturer. Other clues in the research report might indicate the likely name of the company, and it then becomes relatively easy to identify the particular post-holder at the time of the research.

In order to hide the identity of people or organisations, the two main strategies are to use either fictitious names or no names at all. Fictional names can be problematic unless they are carefully chosen, and yet referring to a person as Ms X or Mr Y can make the research report sound very formal, if not awkward. There is really no easy solution. Perhaps the best strategy is to make it clear in the introduction to the research report that you have done your best to hide the identity of your respondents, and that you have done this because of your respect for their privacy. Such a statement might be as follows:

ANONYMITY

The author of this report is very grateful to those people who have given of their time to act as respondents. In order to respect their privacy, they have all been referred to in this report by fictitious names.

Data protection

We live in an age in which information and data about all kinds of things are freely available. However, just because data is freely available does not mean that it is not protected.

It is probably best here to distinguish between primary data collected by yourself, and secondary data which is already in existence. In the former case, you will generally be safe in collecting data, provided that you have permission to do so at a particular location. As long as you have permission of access, then because the data you collect did not (by definition) exist previously, you are probably safe in retaining 'ownership' of that data.

The problem tends to arise with secondary data which was originally collected for some other purpose. For example, if a company has developed guidelines for producing quotations for contracts, that information may be available within the company, but presumably it would be frowned upon if it were disclosed elsewhere. Educational institutions may collect a variety of student-enrolment data, and this may be readily available across a computer network. However, the college would almost certainly regard this as sensitive, or indeed confidential, information, and would not want it to be divulged elsewhere. Published data will almost definitely be subject to copyright law, and permission would have to be obtained before it could be used.

The general rule with secondary data is that it would normally 'belong' to the person who collected and published it, and therefore permission would have to be obtained before it could be used.

—— Publication of findings ——

Ethical issues involving the publication of research findings overlap many of those concerns discussed earlier in the chapter, including the need to protect the privacy of respondents. Nevertheless, publication in some form remains a cornerstone of the research process, for it ensures that research moves from being a private to a public activity as the researcher submits the data and findings of the research to the scrutiny of others. Publication is part of the important system of checks and balances, which helps to bring the essential element of objectivity to the research process.

The term 'publication' can involve a range of types of dissemination, including:

- journalistic articles in magazines or newspapers;
- academic-journal articles;
- books.

They all share the common feature that they can bring an account of the research to a potentially wide readership. In principle, this is also true of research dissertations for university degrees, because these are usually kept in an academic library to which members of the public have access. Dissertations are normally classed as 'unpublished', although in terms of ethics they raise many of the same issues as published works. Despite the fact that they are normally read and consulted only by students, they are in principle open to scrutiny by members of the public who may use the university library for reference purposes.

In one sense, there is no reason why a published research account should be different in terms of standards and presentation to sound, well-designed research which is not published. Good research, it may be argued, is good research. However, it is important to be careful, particularly in terms of any possible misrepresentation of individuals or organisations. When you are on the verge of publishing a research report, it is worth asking yourself such questions as:

- Has anyone been misrepresented in any way in this report?
- If people are named or identified, have they given their permission?
- Has the data been inadvertently distorted in any way?
- Have any personal prejudices been admitted into the research?
- Is there any reasonable way in which the respondents could be identified?
- Have all reasonable steps been taken to secure the anonymity of the respondents?

These questions are often very difficult to answer, because it is not always clear when appropriate precautions have been taken. One sensible step is to ask the advice of one or two professional colleagues. Sometimes we get too close to a research project to be able to judge impartially what we have written, and the steps which we have taken. Sometimes our colleagues or friends can see things more clearly. Often they may be willing to allow their names to be noted in the publication as having been consulted.

It is also possible to include a discussion in the report which explains some of the steps you have taken to consider the feelings of others. Even if someone should later object to what you have written, at least you have indicated your sensitivity to such ethical issues. An analysis of ethical issues in research is contained in May (1993, Chapter 3) and Burgess (1993, Chapter 9) – see the 'Further reading' section.

NEW CONCEPTS

Ethics
Informed consent

Respondent anonymity

METHODS FOR COLLECTING DATA

6

DOCUMENTARY RESEARCH

Using existing data

It is often thought that research must involve the collection of new data. Possible examples include, interview recordings or questionnaire responses. However, this is not necessarily so, because we are surrounded by enormous quantities of potential data which can be used in research investigations. We live in a world society which accumulates a large quantity of documentary information in both paper and computer records. If you can turn this kind of information to your advantage, then it will probably save you considerable time in your research project. There are two main approaches to using existing data:

- to examine data which is available, and then to build a research project around that data;
- to develop a research design, and then to seek out any existing data which may be of help.

The problem with the latter approach is that you simply may not find the exact type of data you want. If you have already defined your research parameters and the variables in which you are interested, then your demands in terms of data may be too narrow to take advantage of the available data.

The first strategy does not, however, involve this kind of difficulty. In this case you might discover, say, that your local public library holds a particularly interesting collection of old newspapers, and you might decide to take advantage of these for a historical study. When planning research, there is nothing wrong to start with the available data. It is often assumed that research designs must first be planned, after which one goes in search of data. It may often be a sensible idea to satisfy yourself that data is available before deciding firmly upon a research design.

Of course, if you build your research plan around existing data, you may not be able to research exactly the topic that you originally wanted. You may have to be flexible and adapt your first idea. It is important within this strategy to ensure that you are investigating a genuine research issue; if you let the available data control the research design too much, the research may not have sufficient precision and focus.

The fact that we are considering data which already exists clearly establishes it as being 'historical' in nature, and this in turn raises a number of important general questions, including:

- When was the data collected?
- Who collected the data?
- For what purpose was it collected?

In the case of much data, it is often very clear when it was collected. Government statistical data often carries the year, or even the month of collection, and this is very important in establishing trends. The situation is obviously similar with articles in newspapers and journals. However, with personal documents, such as diaries, it may not be evident when they were written; conclusions about the date may have to be drawn from references to events, or to meetings with contemporaries. In general, the dating of material is very important, because it relates the documents to contemporary people and events, and enables the researcher to place the documents in an appropriate historical sequence.

The question of who prepared the documents in the first place, or of who collected the data which is included in documents, is a very important matter. Whenever a person collects data, the process of data collection reflects something of the individual involved. Even with carefully planned surveys involving trained interviewers there can never be a complete guarantee that the questions are asked in a standard form. There is always some variation in the way in which questions are asked, even if this only involves a different tone of voice.

When we use documents derived from journalism, we are obviously very interested in knowing how the article was researched and written. We are only too aware of the way in which a single contemporary event can be portrayed very differently in different newspapers. Journalists perceive and report on an event in their own way, partly because of their own individual perspective, and partly because of the way in which their newspapers expect them to write. It is also, of course, very often difficult to know how a journalist collected the information upon which an article is based.

Documents, we can assume, are always written for a purpose, and it is often very revealing to know about that purpose. Take the case of diaries, for example. Some people write these as purely personal documents, and do not intend them ever to be read by others. There are other types of diary, however, whose writer either does not mind if it is read by others, or perhaps specifically intends it for public consumption. Politicians, for example, may keep a diary or notebook during their term of office with the specific intention of editing it into book form when they retire.

In such cases, the document can only be read and analysed in the context of the purpose for which it was written. We would expect a private diary to contain much more personal thoughts and revelations than a 'public' diary. We also might be somewhat cautious about interpreting the writing in a 'public' diary if we suspected that events were being carefully presented for public consumption. This is a difficult area, and the researcher has no easy task when interpreting the way in which a diarist decided to record events.

We will now turn to a closer examination of different forms of documents used in research and we will start by considering **personal documents**.

Personal documents

Many of us accumulate a great number of documents during the course of a lifetime, and while we may assume that these are fairly ordinary and not likely to interest others, this may not be the case. Sometimes documents which may not be very unusual on their own become much more significant when compared with a number of similar documents belonging to other people.

Personal documents were typically prepared for some individual purpose, rather than for a public audience. As such we might include the following types of material:

- diaries;
- notebooks;
- drawings and sketches;
- collections of photographs;
- letters (both to and from the respondent);
- autobiographies.

These kinds of material are particularly useful when compiling case studies or ethnographies of people or social contexts. They are typically characterised by an interest value and richness which may not so easily be found in survey research, for example. Such documents frequently give us an insight into the innermost thoughts, hopes and aspirations of people, and this kind of data is often the only way in which we can investigate these matters.

The unique nature of personal documents often makes their interpretation difficult, if not problematic. Reliability and validity are the key questions here. We must ask ourselves whether a second researcher would interpret the material in quite the same way as ourselves. Secondly, we must consider whether the conclusions and interpretations we are drawing are valid.

The use of triangulation is a very important strategy here. If a letter from the person being researched suggests one conclusion, then we should try to find letters from other individuals which support this.

Although the kinds of document listed above are very varied, there are a number of significant and common questions which they raise in the mind of the researcher, including:

- Are the documents genuinely the work of the supposed author?
- Can the documents be accurately dated?
- Is it clear where the documents were created?
- What was the prime purpose in creating the documents?
- Are there restrictions on the use and reporting of the documents?

People create personal documents for all kinds of reasons. Sometimes they create them in the hope and expectation that their contemporaries will read them. Alternatively, they may make no attempt to encourage others to read them. However, sometimes people make every attempt to ensure the survival of their documents, thus perhaps seeking to create a kind of immortality.

Nevertheless, a significant question with regard to personal documents is why some survive to become data while others do not. Autobiographies are an interesting case in point. An examination of the autobiography section of a public library shows that most are the work of individuals who are already famous for one reason or another. The public generally wants to read about people who are well known. This very form of selectivity ensures that those who are already famous have their lives recorded in print, while only a very small number of those who are not well known manage to publish their autobiography.

One great virtue of personal documents, including autobiographies, is that they are independent of any influence exerted by the researcher. Researchers can at least know that they have not affected their production. However, even though the data is extremely rich, careful analysis is still required, particularly in terms of drawing conclusions which can be supported as valid.

—————— Statistical data ——————

Quantitative data exists in profusion in our society. Numerical data is to be found in advertisements, newspaper articles, school reports, literature from banks and insurance companies, and in government publications. Any of this can be put to interesting use for research purposes. The only possible problem is that if your research design is fairly precise, with hypotheses to test, then you may be lucky to find relevant data.

The major problem with statistical data which we have not collected ourselves is that we cannot be certain exactly how it was collected, or what questions were asked. Kane (1985, p.115; see the 'Further reading' section) emphasises this point:

In using archival sources, it is essential that you understand their limitations. Most documentary information is collected for purposes entirely unrelated to those to which researchers put them.

Some of the data may even have been amassed from other sources, and so may not have been collected from original observations or measurements. Even if the data was collected by original measurement, it is very important how the questions were asked. For example, consider the following types of question which might form part of a questionnaire.

1	Do you go abroad for your holidays?	Yes/No
2	Have you ever been unemployed?	Yes/No
3	Do you have a driving licence?	Yes/No

Superficially, these questions seem straightforward, but as we begin to try to answer them we may become less and less sure. In Question 1 we may be uncertain whether the Isle of Wight or Isle of Man count as going abroad from England. Does going to England count as going abroad from Scotland? Does going to Alaska count as going abroad from the United States? We cannot be sure that everyone will interpret the question in the same way. The word 'unemployed' in Question 2 may seem sufficiently precise, but it is subject to different interpretations. If someone has finished a full-time course of education and training, and is seeking a job, does that count as being unemployed? What level of part-time work counts as being unemployed? If someone works for a charity and receives only nominal payment, does that count as being unemployed? With a question such as this, people will make up their own minds about how to answer it, and this will clearly affect the value of the final data. In Question 3 it is similarly unclear whether a provisional driving licence or a motorcycle licence is adequate reason for answering 'yes'.

Statistical data, then, must be treated with the same caution as other data. It is important to realise that just because it is in numerical form, it is not necessarily any more valid than other data. Before we use such documents we should try to clarify the social setting in which the information was collected, and also investigate the data-collection process.

Official records

Official records of government departments and of formal institutions such as hospitals and colleges are extremely useful sources of research data. Such documents exist in very large numbers, and are characteristic of the large bureaucracies in which they are found. Such large organisations depend upon the passing of precise information from one department to another. In the past, communication was largely paper-based, but now electronic methods such as e-mail are coming into common use. Examples of such documents include:

- agendas and minutes of meetings;
- policy proposals;
- memoranda;
- post or job specifications;
- instructions to colleagues;
- circulars providing general institutional information;
- invoices.

The first problem with such documents is one of access. Whether or not you work in the organisation from which they originated there are likely to be problems involved with using such documents. You will probably need to ask permission to use them, and even then you should be very cautious about confidentiality. People will typically be named in such documents, and some of the information contained in them may be personal.

One important aspect of official records is the extent to which they are socially constructed. A good example of this is the record of a formal or official meeting. The process of creating the official record is fairly lengthy, and there are several stages in which the interpretation of events by individuals can impinge upon the official record. The normal process is that someone acts as secretary during the meeting and takes notes from which the minutes will be later constructed. If the secretary is also an active member of the meeting, and contributes to the debate, this is a possible source of error in the notes. For example, once the secretary has finished speaking, he or she will start to write notes on those comments, and cannot concentrate on what is being said by others. Quite apart from this, however, there is the possibility that a secretary will write more detailed notes on the things that he or she deems to be interesting. This bias may be reflected in the final minutes.

Once the meeting is over, there may be a delay of several days before the secretary prepares a set of draft minutes from the notes. There is obviously a possible source of error here: partly because of the delay, and partly through the selective process of interpreting the notes.

The draft minutes will then normally be shown to the chair of the meeting, who may amend or edit them depending upon his or her recollection of the meeting. The chair may not have kept notes, but will still change the draft minutes if he or she feels it necessary. Finally, at the next meeting, which may be some time away, the minutes will be submitted to the scrutiny of those present. Not all of the members of the original meeting may be present at this meeting. Those who are able to do so, will comment on the accuracy of the minutes, and the latter will be approved as a true record, either with or without any alterations. Once approved, the minutes become the 'confirmed' record of the meeting, and as such pass into posterity.

There is a tendency to regard minutes as in some way representing 'reality'. In fact they are a socially constructed account, which may reflect many of the perspectives of those who have helped in their construction. It is very important to look at official documents in this way, and to ask oneself questions about the process whereby they came into being. Only in this way can we begin to draw conclusions about their validity, and the extent to which they reflect 'reality'.

——— Historical documents ———

Researchers who use historical documents tend to make a different distinction between primary and secondary sources to that made by social scientists outlined in Chapter 1. Naturally it is impossible for historians to step into the past and collect, say, interview data from key figures; we cannot go back to 1066 and ask William of Normandy how he was feeling just before embarking for England.

Primary sources therefore tend to be defined as those documents originating roughly from the time of the event being studied. The perfect type of primary source would be a descriptive account of an event, perhaps a battle, written just afterwards by a combatant or observer. A secondary source, on the other hand, would be a more recent discussion and evaluation of the available primary sources describing an event. Secondary documents would typically be written by professional historians who are skilled in the analysis of data.

So-called primary documents do vary a great deal, however. Some may clearly have been produced by people who were not present at the described events. This would of necessity be true of those historical periods when reading and writing were not widespread skills. Documents would be produced by the literate few who would rely as far as possible on first-hand accounts. The distinction between primary and secondary sources is thus only approximate, but still of great value in enabling us to assess the validity of research conclusions.

A fairly obvious aspect of historical documentary research is that it is not normally possible to generate new data. One has to make do with what is available. Occasionally a new document may be located, but generally it is a matter of trying to analyse an existing document in a new or novel way. This certainly applies to documents from earlier historical periods.

In more recent times, however, it has become possible to generate more data, particularly by using techniques such as **oral history** or **life history**. Essentially these use living respondents who are asked to think back to periods which they have lived through. As Armstrong (1987, p.8; see the 'Further reading' section) suggests:

> Thus, the life-history method assigns significance and value to the person's 'own story', or to interpretations that people place on their own experiences as an explanation for their own behaviour.

There are a number of techniques which may be used to construct oral-history documents:

- respondents may be asked during informal, taped interviews about events that they have experienced. These tapes can be transcribed;
- respondents may write their own accounts;
- the researcher may talk to the respondent, write an account in the third person, and finally ask the respondent to verify it for accuracy.

In addition, when people are engaged in relaxed conversation about events that they have witnessed it sometimes emerges that they possess historical, personal documents to which they may not attach much significance, but which are of great interest to the researcher.

Oral- and life-history documents provide enormously rich data which frequently contrast with the 'official' accounts of historical events.

They can provide the views of participants in history, rather than those of professional historians. They may present a sometimes restricted and subjective account, but nevertheless one that reflects an intensity and variety of experience.

—— Newspapers and journals ——

Newspapers, magazines and journals present a ready source of data for research, but nevertheless data which should be used with caution. A number of questions arise from such data – questions which should not necessarily result in rejecting the data, but in at least thinking clearly about matters of validity.

A fairly clear issue with regard to journalism is whether the journalist actually witnessed the events being described, or has written a composite account based on other evidence. The exact status of the journalism will obviously affect how it can be treated as research data. If it is a composite account, it may include verbatim extracts from eye-witness accounts, and in this case the article may be useful as data. On the other hand, if it consists exclusively of commentary by the author, then one can suppose that a good deal of the journalist's perspective and world view has been superimposed upon the material.

The question of the ideological content of journalistic documents is clearly crucial. **Ideology** can operate at a number of levels, and is less of a problem in research terms when the author acknowledges the nature of their ideological commitment, and the way in which it may have affected their writing. It becomes much more significant when any ideology is not admitted, and when there is no attempt to reflect upon the influence of the journalist's world view.

A crucial aspect of any journalistic account being considered for research is the background decision-making with regard to such questions as:

- Why was this event selected for reporting?
- How was its degree of prominence in the newspaper established?
- Was the issue covered by an editorial?

The 'news' is not, in sociological terms, 'given' or 'real'. It is most certainly a human construct. Decisions are taken about the promotion of certain 'stories'. The relative importance and significance attached to events is a feature of a human value system and world view. In understanding documents as research data, it is essential to reflect upon this process.

Company and organisational records

Finally, we will consider the use of documents which are generated by commercial companies. Commercial organisations disseminate a large amount of documentary information, often in the form of marketing material for their products, or of sales information or annual reports. Understandably, one would be surprised if they did not emphasise the strengths and successes of the company. Such documents are useful as data, but must clearly be read in their context of presenting a commercial image.

Documents which are presented for external consumption can be contrasted with those internal documents whose function is to convey information or decisions within a company. Both external and internal documents are valuable data. Internal documents can range from memoranda conveying routine information to papers discussing confidential policies. It may be very difficult to get permission either to see or to use many internal documents, and this can make questions of sampling almost irrelevant. In that sense, researchers must make the best of what they are given. However, this is not to say that we should not think very analytically about the status and validity of such documents.

An interesting aspect of documents within commercial organisations is the fact that some survive and others are destroyed. An employee often decides many times in a single day either to retain or to discard a document. The grounds for reaching that decision make an interesting subject for study. The individual might ask such questions as:

- Do I possess other sources of this same information?
- Is this information significant to my job role?
- Is this information currently important in the organisation?
- Might this information become relevant in the future?
- Does this document record an issue upon which I should have an opinion?

This is only a brief indication of some of the questions which enable us to decide how to treat a document. Should it be kept or shredded? Should it be passed horizontally or vertically in the hierarchy? The conclusions which employees come to frequently affect the survival or non-survival of documents. Such matters are significant in research, because the history of a document and the ideas which it contains are a function of the social context within which it arises. Such processes are always of interest and significance in social-science research.

Summary

To summarise, then, researchers use documents as data because:

- the data can sometimes not be collected in any other way;
- a lot of time can be saved;
- a large amount of detailed data may be available;
- the data can help to develop a research idea;
- the data can be qualitative or quantitative, and can lend itself to varied types of analysis.

NEW CONCEPTS

Ideology	Oral history
Life history	Personal documents
Official records	

7

SURVEY RESEARCH

Purpose of a survey

A survey is conducted in order to collect data from a large number of respondents who may be geographically dispersed. The amount of data collected from each individual respondent may be relatively small, but because the total number of respondents is large, a considerable quantity of information is usually collected during a survey. This approach to research can be readily contrasted with some qualitative approaches, such as case studies and ethnographies which involve the collection of complex, in-depth data from a much smaller group of respondents. The contrasting approaches tell us different things about individuals and social situations. Each is suited to particular research problems.

Surveys are employed to measure:

- the extent to which an attitude, lifestyle or social custom is present in a population;
- the development of trends in a population;
- the characteristics of a particular population, e.g. those individuals in a single profession or type of employment.

It should be noted that surveys are not only carried out on populations of people. We can survey inanimate objects, such as cars, houses or factories. A researcher might be interested in the number of cars with defective tyres which are on the road, or in the proportion of houses of a certain age which have had double glazing fitted.

Surveys are conducted regularly throughout society in order to achieve a number of specific goals. One of the most familiar types of survey is when government departments or agencies collect information about the general population as part of a census. This information is crucial in ensuring that government policy can be based upon valid social and economic data. Surveys are also important in industry and business because they enable managers to make informed policy decisions. Scientists and academics employ surveys to try to resolve what may initially be primarily academic problems, but which have important implications. Studies of, say, the accumulation of toxic substances in various ecosystems and food chains may start off as academic research, but this kind of data may ultimately have important implications for human health.

Medical researchers use surveys to monitor the distribution of certain clinical conditions in the population. By studying the survey's results, they are then in a position to judge whether a particular occurrence of the condition is typical of the population as a whole, or if it represents a localised, abnormal event. Indeed surveys are crucial in many aspects of medical and health studies, and can be used to monitor habits such as smoking, and also to assess customer satisfaction with medical provision in, say, hospitals.

— Principles of questionnaire design —

In this section we will consider the general aspects of questionnaire design, while in the next section different approaches to writing questions will be considered. There are two main types of questionnaire:

- the **interview questionnaire** (administered by the researcher);
- the **self-completion questionnaire** (distributed by mail, or by hand).

Aspects of design are fundamentally different in the two cases. The interview questionnaire is designed to be used by the researcher. The latter reads out the questions and notes the replies given by the respondents. It is important that the design is such that the researcher can read the questionnaire in a standard form to each respondent. This is particularly significant when teams of researchers are using the same questionnaire. The design of the questionnaire should easily enable the researcher to record responses, and to be consistent in the delivery of questions. Sometimes interview question-naires may be used in busy, noisy situations, such as in marketing survey research in town centres. It is not always easy to concentrate on the questions under such circumstances, and a clear, simple design can be a great help.

The interview questionnaire is in many ways quite simple to admin-ister, because of the very fact that the researcher is present. If, for example, the respondent provides an answer which is not one of the possible coded responses offered, then the researcher can place it in the appropriate category. This kind of interaction is, of course, not possible with the self-completion questionnaire. This latter type of questionnaire is posted to the respondent, or is delivered by hand, and is completed by the respondent without any intervention by the researcher. It follows from this that the questionnaire must be self-standing and capable of being easily understood by the respondent. Quite clearly, a good deal of careful design work must be carried out to ensure that the instructions are clearly understood, and that the questions are unambiguous. Despite this, there are a number of advantages to this type of survey.

The interview survey is very costly and time-consuming, in the sense that considerable input by the research team is necessary. However, once a self-completion questionnaire has been designed, it can be posted to a very large number of respondents. Naturally, not all of these will respond, and a carefully-worded letter must be drafted to try to encourage participation in the survey. This type of survey is very useful for reaching a geographically dispersed sample of people. It is normally difficult, if not impossible, to survey distant locations, and travel costs may be prohibitive. **Postal surveys** enable you to target respondents precisely, and to at least establish contact with them. A personal telephone call may not result in contact with a member of the sample population, whereas the mailed questionnaire will at least reach their address.

The self-completion questionnaire must be visually attractive in terms of its layout. The respondent must feel that it would be inter-esting and worthwhile to complete. Many of the respondents may not be familiar with form completion, and they should not be put off by an unduly complex layout, or by complicated instructions. It probably helps if the early questions are straightforward, in order to reassure respondents. A number of design strategies can be employed to make the questionnaire more user friendly. For example, different type fonts can be used to distinguish separate parts of the questionnaire; this is especially important in the case of headings, instructions, questions and response boxes. Spacing is also very important. A small text size and tight spacing between lines make the questionnaire difficult to read. Even though it is more costly in terms of paper, generous spacing and a large print size are probably more productive in the long run.

Writing questions

If a questionnaire is to be successful in terms of obtaining responses, then it must hold the interest of respondents. This is true of interview questionnaires, but especially so in the case of self-completion questionnaires. In the latter case, there is no interviewer to sustain the interest of the respondent. The layout of the questionnaire, and the content, pacing and sequence of the questions must therefore help to motivate the respondent to complete the questionnaire.

It is very easy to ask rather frustrating questions in a questionnaire. For example, most of us find it difficult to carry facts, figures and dates in our heads, particularly if we are not being asked for them every day. Consider the following questions:

- How old is your car?
- In which year did you move into your present house?
- When were you appointed to your present job? (Month and year).

Such questions are basically straightforward, but if the age or event is more than several years in the past, it may take considerable thought to work out the exact answer. If respondents have to work too hard at answering questions they can easily lose their motivation and interest. In addition, respondents are often being asked to complete questionnaires when they are either tired or very busy, and in either case they may not have the patience to work out such answers.

Questions should therefore be very simple in terms of their structure, and should be easy to read and understand. The respondent should not need to reread the question in order to understand it. The vocabulary should be non-technical.

The possible responses to questions should be coded to help analysis later. It may be necessary to include an 'other' category, in order to include alternative responses to the main options. Another possibility is to provide a space in which respondents can note any alternative responses. These can then be post-coded by the interviewer or researcher.

The writing of good questionnaire questions is a complex art, and a lot of factors should be taken into account when doing so. An important aim is to avoid confusing the respondent, and there are a number of precautions which can be taken in this respect. Questions which pose alternatives are frequently difficult to answer. For example, a student may be asked:

> Do you think that a teacher's main job is to pass on knowledge, or do you think that it should be to interest pupils in the subject?

It is very difficult to give a simple 'yes' or 'no' response to this. Both functions are very important aspects of a teacher's job, and it is difficult to say that one is more important than the other. Perhaps a more meaningful way of approaching the issue would be to consider the different ways in which teachers convey knowledge, and the different ways in which they inculcate interest. This might result in a question such as:

> Here is a list of different ways in which a teacher may pass on knowledge. Tick the one which you, as a student, prefer.
> 1 A reading list for you to consult.   - - -
> 2 A talk or lecture.   - - -
> 3 Hand-outs.   - - -
> 4 A practical investigation or exercise.   - - -
> 5 A video and accompanying notes.   - - -
> 6 Other, please state.   - - -
>
> . . . .

In this case, of course, respondents may feel that they are being forced to pick one of the options, despite the fact that their choice really depends upon the particular learning situation. However, there is a rather greater degree of precision inherent in this type of question.

It can also be confusing when a number of questions are grouped together as one. The questionnaire writer may do this in order to save space, but the result is almost inevitably a confusing question. For example:

What is the make, model, engine capacity and age of your present car?

Not only is the question asking for a variety of information in a single answer, but it is making an assumption about the respondent – that he or she owns a car. It would be much better to ask such questions as:

Do you drive a car?   Yes - - - No - - -
Who is the registered owner of the car?

A Yourself   - - -
B Your spouse   - - -
C A company or business - - -
D Other, please specify   - - -

. . . .

What is the make of the car? . . . .

It is very easy to make assumptions about the respondent. For example, consider the question:

What is your favourite television programme shown before 9.00 p.m.?

This assumes that the respondent actually owns a television; secondly, watches it before 9.00 p.m.; and thirdly, watches it sufficiently frequently to form a judgement on the programmes. Again, it is preferable to start with short questions which establish the background of the specific respondent in terms of both owning a television, and watching it.

Sometimes a researcher is tempted to ask a question about a possible event in the future, such as:

If you were planning a holiday, where would you go?

Such a question may inherently possess low reliability and validity. The respondent may choose to answer it from a purely personal point of view, or may be thinking about the preferences of their spouse and family. If asked the question on two separate occasions, the same respondent may answer from a different perspective. It is better to ask questions which are more definite and precisely worded.

Finally, it may be possible to elicit biased responses because of the way in which questions are worded. Some questions may suggest a particular type of response. These are so-called 'leading questions'.

Do you think that it is only fair that we should all carry an organ-donor card?

The use of the phrase 'only fair' may tend to focus our attention on the plight of people needing an organ transplant. The result is that there could be a tendency to answer in the affirmative. However, the issues surrounding organ donation are very complex indeed, and they should really be explored by a series of precise questions. Leading questions reduce the validity of the data, and great care should be taken to avoid writing them into questionnaires.

The pilot study

It is seldom possible to identify all the design faults and failings in the wording of questions when preparing a questionnaire. As Oppenheim (1992, p.47; see the 'Further reading' section) writes:

> Questionnaires do not emerge fully fledged; they have to be created or adapted, fashioned and developed to maturity after many abortive test flights.

The design task is so complex that it is difficult even when a team of researchers is involved. It is much better to try out the questionnaire with an initial sample of respondents, and to observe the difficulties which they experience in completing it. This type of procedure is known as a **pilot study**.

In some cases, problems with the questionnaire can be identified by simple observation. For example, if a number of respondents in an interview survey all ask for clarification about a particular question, then this question can be reworded. It is usually quite easy in an interview survey to observe difficulties with the questionnaire. These might be as follows:

- the researcher may have trouble following the guidance notes;
- the researcher may not be able to code all of the replies to some questions;
- respondents may appear to lose interest part of the way through the questionnaire;
- respondents may have to think for too long about questions, which results in them apparently losing interest in the survey.

It is also possible to ask respondents about their experience of the questionnaire once it is completed. In the case of self-completion questionnaires, collecting such pilot data is more difficult. However, some clues do emerge simply through the style in which the questionnaire is completed. Some respondents may not have followed the instructions properly; if a significant number have made the same procedural mistakes, then this may be the result of the imprecise phrasing of the instructions. It can also be useful to ask a sample of respondents to work through a self-completion questionnaire with the researcher present, and to comment on any imprecise or ambiguous questions. The researcher can then reflect on their suggestions, and if necessary, make amendments accordingly.

Sampling methods

The purpose of a sample is to represent as closely as possible the characteristics of the survey population, i.e. the group of people being studied. The extent to which it is representative will depend upon the size of the sample, and the manner in which it is selected. Generally speaking, the larger the sample, the more it is likely to be representative of the population. In addition, probability samples are much better at being representative than non-probability samples.

In all sampling, it is crucial for the researcher to define the terms employed in describing the population and sample. It is very imprecise, for example, to speak of a population of students, without specifying more clearly the type of students. In the student context, it may be important to specify the following:

- whether students are full time or part time;
- whether they are studying at college or university;
- the subject area being studied;
- the age range;
- whether they are studying on secondment from work.

In some surveys, it may be very difficult to know whom to contact for data. For example, in a survey of businesses, it may not be obvious which post-holder should be contacted. Different businesses may not use the same role descriptions: for instance, if it is decided to contact the export departments of businesses, some businesses may have an export manager, whereas others may subsume those duties under another job description; yet other firms may concentrate exclusively on the domestic market. Unless the most accurate and commonly used job description is employed when directing questionnaires there may be a very low response rate. The problem may not be solved by sending questionnaires to, say, the managing director, hoping that this will result in some consistency in the type of respondent. It is possible that some of the questionnaires will be delegated to junior colleagues for response, and that there may be no consistency in the approaches to responses.

In many surveys, certain techniques must be used to make the sample procedure practicable. For example, consider a survey of, say, amateur cricket players. There will probably be no national listing of these, although we might be able to compile a list from the membership lists of all such cricket clubs. A more practical approach would be to obtain a list of cricket clubs, and then to take a random sample of those, perhaps within a restricted geographical area. Lists of players could then be compiled from the current teams, for example, and a final random sample could be taken from those lists. This would at least result in a manageable sample.

A final difficulty with sampling is that certain groups of people are not evenly distributed throughout the population. For example, teachers, firemen and policemen exist in numbers roughly proportionate to the size of the population in an area. In other words, the larger the population of an area, the more teachers, firemen and policemen will generally be needed. Many occupational groups are not distributed in this way, however. Fishermen, agricultural workers, dockers and members of the armed forces are likely to live in areas determined by their occupation. Some ethnic and religious groups live in areas often determined by earlier patterns of migration and settlement. These issues are important considerations when planning a survey, and when determining the survey population and sampling strategy.

Response rates

Obtaining a reasonable **response rate** becomes an important issue particularly where postal questionnaires are concerned. Potential respondents may not be as excited about a research project as the research team, and so may need persuasion to complete and return the questionnaire.

The researcher can take certain steps to be as helpful as possible to the respondents. The enclosure of a stamped addressed envelope certainly helps. It is also useful to consider the timing of sending out questionnaires. Ask yourself if respondents are likely to be especially busy at the time when they receive the survey documents. Different categories of people may be busy at distinct times of the year: July and August may not be a sensible time to survey university students, for example, as they may either be travelling abroad or working at vacation jobs, perhaps away from home.

The covering letter should be carefully worded, but should not be too long. Respondents are always likely to be busy, and may not have the patience to read a long letter. It should explain very briefly the nature and purpose of the survey, and should reassure respondents that confidentiality will be maintained. It could include a brief statement explaining why you consider the research to be important, and saying that it would be very helpful if you could get replies from everyone. You may want to draw attention to the stamped addressed envelope, and to give a date by which you would hope to receive a response.

When that date has passed, you may decide to send reminders to those who have not replied. A code-number system on the original questionnaires will enable a list of non-respondents to be drawn up. It may be a good idea to include another copy of the questionnaire in the reminder envelope, just in case the original has been lost. It may probably also be worth drawing the respondent's attention again to the importance of the research, and to the advantages of obtaining a good response rate.

Encouraging people to reply to postal questionnaires is not easy, and the strategies which work for one group of people may not work for another. You should try to put yourself in the position of the respondent, and should think about those factors which would motivate you to return a questionnaire.

Summary

To summarise, researchers use surveys because:

- a lot of data can be collected by means of a single questionnaire;
- data can be collected from a large number of people;
- respondents can be contacted when they are at a distance, or even overseas;
- data can be quantified;
- surveys are relatively efficient in terms of time.

NEW CONCEPTS

Interview questionnaire	Response rate
Pilot study	Self-completion questionnaire
Postal survey	

8

CASE-STUDY RESEARCH

— Characteristics of the case study —

A case study involves a detailed exploration of a single instance of, or example of, something. All kinds of individuals or social groups, institutions or events can be regarded as 'cases' worthy of study. Examples of possible case studies include:

- an individual who assumes the role of managing director of a large organisation;
- an all-night coffee bar located in a large city;
- a change in strategy for the teaching of reading in a primary school;
- a group of people who join a religious community.

The first case study is of an individual person, and could focus upon the feelings and reactions of that person in the new role. There might also be an investigation of the attitudes of the other staff to the new personality, and to the changes in policy which are initiated. You might also describe the general context of the organisation, and try to provide an account of the interaction of the new chief executive with the entire organisation.

The second case study is an example of an institution – a coffee bar. If you were carrying out this type of case study, you would probably be very interested in its changing clientele throughout the day and night. You might also be interested in recording the relationship between the café owner and the customers. During the 24-hour period, different social groups will probably gather at the café, and you may well try to provide an account of these groups. The data is linked together by the focus upon the coffee bar as a single institution.

The third example is a case study of a policy change in the teaching of reading. This case study could describe the nature of the change in strategy, and the apparent results in pupil performance. It could also involve the gathering of data from parents and teachers, recording their reactions to the new teaching strategy.

The final example is of a case study of a social group, and of their reactions when joining a religious community. The religious order could be described, along with the reactions of the existing members of the order to the new members. The main focus of the study, however, would be the group of new members, and the ways in which they interact with each other and with the community.

Case studies can thus consist of:

- an individual;
- an institution;
- a policy change;
- a social group.

A case study is usually selected because it reflects an important current issue. It may also be that each case selected for study is, to some extent, typical of a general **category**. For instance, in the examples given above, the new managing director may perhaps be typical of other people who assume positions of responsibility in large organisations; moreover, the group of people joining a religious community may, to some degree, be typical of other groups joining a closed community.

The case study adopts a very different perspective to research when compared with the survey or the experiment. There is no attempt to control variables, or to gather data from a carefully selected sample. The purpose is rather to build up a very detailed picture of a single case, and of the interactions taking place within that case.

A case study of an individual will typically focus upon some significant aspects of the current life of that individual, and will in addition relate these to past events and experiences. There will also be an attempt to explore the social interaction between the individual and the current context. Different issues can be explored by collecting data in a variety of ways, and such methodological triangulation can help to establish the degree of the data's internal validity.

The same is true of case studies of organisations. The purpose is to explore some of the multifaceted aspects of the organisation, using data from different sources. In this way, a much more sophisticated and rich picture is constructed than would be created from survey data.

—————— Identifying a subject ——————

The selection of a case study is a complicated process, or at least it can be. On one level, you could make a quick decision and simply choose an individual or organisation to research. However, if the study is to have any external validity, then the choice of a case to investigate should be made after a good deal of careful thought.

As with most types of research, access to the object of the enquiry is one of the main initial concerns. If the case study is an individual, you need to consider whether the person would be willing to give up a possibly large amount of time to help with the research. You also need to think about your own work schedule and time commitments. Case-study research can often be very time-consuming because of the large amount of observation involved. It is best to think carefully about all of these factors before you approach the individual.

In the case of organisations, the question of access may revolve around the willingness of the organisation to submit itself to public scrutiny. When approaching an organisation, it is not always easy to know which role-holder to ask for permission for your research. If you approach someone at one level in an organisation, and this turns out to be an inappropriate level in the hierarchy, then it may prejudice the gaining of access through someone else.

If the case for study is intended to be a group of people, then the gaining of access may be complicated by the fact that some may be willing to co-operate but others may be unwilling. Access may be easier if it is proposed that the data is collected at times when the group is assembled together, rather than trying to contact individuals separately. In many ways, these issues of access are very similar to those faced in ethnographic research.

Questions of access are also inseparable from matters of research ethics. This is particularly so where individuals are concerned. If a person agrees to be the subject of a case study, then it is in effect an agreement to make public what otherwise would be regarded as private information. It is clearly important that the person understands fully what is being undertaken, is briefed on the uses to which the research will be put, and is reassured that the research can be ended on request at any point.

Quite apart from the issue of access, another major concern when selecting a case for study is that it should be likely to provide data to help you to address some of your research issues. In the case of the study of the coffee bar mentioned above, one of the purposes of the study might be to investigate the different social groups who congregate there at particular times in the day. Suppose, for the sake of example, that the first coffee bar chosen exhibits a fairly uniform client group throughout the 24-hour period – it might then be considered unsuitable as a case study. Another coffee bar, which attracts a wider range of customers, might be regarded as being a more interesting case. To some extent, the selection of a case depends upon whether the research design assumes a single case study, or perhaps a series of case studies. In the former situation, it might be felt that the most appropriate case is one which possesses the greatest number of interesting or unusual features.

Case-study research overlaps a good deal with several other research traditions. It is clear that there can be a close relationship with ethnographic research from what has been considered above; the use of a coffee bar as a 'case' is very close in research terms to writing an ethnography of a coffee bar. In addition, case-study research can overlap considerably with policy research. In the latter type of research, the case to be considered could be a new policy initiative in an organisation. The case study will involve an analysis of the stages leading up to the innovation, and the social context of the policy change. In addition, there will be a description and an analysis of the consequences of the development, and perhaps also recommendations regarding possible future policy changes. Case studies of this type are very often investigated by a research team, because of the many different aspects of the policy initiative which require exploration.

Types of method used

The case study does not presuppose any particular type of data to be collected, or any specific data-collection procedure; a wide range of methods is traditionally used. However, it has to be said that qualitative methods in general are probably more typically associated with case-study research. Quantitative methods, associated as they are with statistical generalisations, are less suited to the case study. However, there will be many instances of case studies in which quantitative data will be not only appropriate, but even essential. Consider the study of a case of an actuarial department of a large insurance company; it may be very difficult to do justice to such a study without collecting statistical data.

A list of all the methods ever used in case studies would probably be very long indeed, but here are some examples of the main types of method which you can employ:

- observation studies – both participant or non-participant;
- interviews;
- conversational recording and analysis;
- photographs and videotaping;
- role-playing.

Observation studies are particularly suited to case-study research because of its need to develop an in-depth picture of the case, and of the social relationships of which it is a part. Non-participant studies can be useful when researching organisations. After you have obtained permission for access, then you can walk around the institution taking notes, watching people at work, and observing social interactions. Once you have been approved as a *bona fide* researcher and have been given access, then there are relatively few ethical dilemmas involved. You can, in a sense, report what you see. There will still remain the need to ensure confidentiality, however.

Participant observation, on the other hand, may well yield richer, and more detailed, data. As you immerse yourself into the case study, be it of social group or organisation, you may have access to data which would normally remain hidden from the non-participant observer. However, ethical issues can arise, particularly when the members of the case being studied do not know that you are a participant-researcher. Such a case involves dilemmas about whether the data should be used, and if so, in what manner.

Interviews are another very useful method for researching case studies, but have the disadvantage that the validity of the data may be reduced by the interaction between the researcher and the respondent. If a case study is being conducted in an institutional setting, those working within it may be rather reluctant to pass comments upon some aspects of their work environment. Imagine a school teacher being asked to comment on the management style of the headteacher, or of a sales executive being asked a question about the company's marketing priorities. In both cases, the interviewees would probably have very definite views on the issues, but may be extremely circumspect in giving those views.

Nevertheless, interviews remain a key strategy for collecting case-study data, and are particularly significant when it is impracticable or impossible to collect observational data. Many social contexts in which human beings are involved are either private, or too sensitive to observe. In some cases, an individual would not wish to be observed, and in others an organisation would withhold its permission. A company, for example, would not want an outsider being present when sensitive matters of corporate finance were being discussed. Individual people, on the other hand, may be perfectly willing to be interviewed about a sensitive issue because they can put their own gloss on events, and can even refuse to discuss certain matters if they are too delicate. In addition, historical events can clearly not be observed, and we must rely on, for example, the personal accounts of those who have experienced the events.

Finally, interview data is absolutely crucial for those case studies which propose to explore the feelings and attitudes of people. Such attributes cannot be directly observed, and clearly have to be explored through questioning and discussion. To some extent, feelings and attitudes can be examined by observing their secondary effects in terms of changes in individual behaviour, but the assumptions and connections made by the researcher may be less than valid.

A very useful technique for exploring case studies is to make a permanent record of some of the transitory events involved, or of the physical surroundings. Audio-tape recording is the traditional means of recording conversation, and can be used while interviews are being held, and the discussions later transcribed. Audio recorders can also be set up in locations in which casual or group conversations may be heard, and can thus create a record of informal, verbal exchanges. In such cases, however, the ethical issues may be more complex than with one-to-one interviews. It is fairly easy to ask one person for their permission to record an interview, but it is much more difficult in practical terms to get the permission of a group. Even harder is obtaining permission to record casual conversation. Imagine that you wanted to research verbal exchanges in a school staff room, or a works canteen, and wished to set up a tape recorder in order to do so. Obtaining permission from everyone who would be likely to be recorded would be difficult. Covert tape recording in such situations is excluded on ethical grounds.

Videotaping is a very useful technique used to obtain a record of the physical environment of a building or institution, and can also be used to record interpersonal exchanges. Videotaping has the great advantage that it records non-verbal communication which, in an interview, for example, may be very significant data. From a research-ethics viewpoint, respondents or participants will almost always require reassurance as to the use to which the videotape will be put. Photographs may be a slightly less intrusive measure, but they clearly cannot capture the wealth of data which it is possible to record with a video recorder. Nevertheless, they may be very useful when recording an aspect of the physical environment in a case study.

Role-playing is not always regarded as a method of data collection in case studies, but can be considered under certain circumstances. For example, you might telephone an organisation with a legitimate enquiry in order to investigate the ways in which enquiries are handled. In a sense, you would be taking on the role of a potential customer. There do not seem to be too many ethical problems involved in such a case, as arguably everyone is a potential customer. However, other types of role-playing designed to investigate how people may respond could be unacceptably intrusive.

—— Using documentary records ——

The data-collection methods described in the previous section all share one characteristic: they are all, to some extent, intrusive upon the social situation. To put this another way, they all disturb the social ecology somewhat. You cannot observe without having some effect upon those observed. You cannot converse without affecting, however slightly, those with whom you talk. Furthermore all of the methods discussed involve the collection of data which is specifically for research purposes.

Documentary records, however, are different, in the sense that they normally already exist for other purposes, and are then employed as data by researchers. There is an extraordinarily wide range of documents available, which can be of use in case studies. Documents can be classified into the following broad types:

● personal records including references, testimonials, school reports, employment histories and curricula vitae;
● official statistics collected by government departments or agencies. These can include census material and data on births, marriages and deaths;
● legal documents/transactions such as contracts, mortgage deeds, loan agreements and court records;
● publicity and marketing material produced by large organisations, such as banks or insurance companies, and also by small companies;
● indexes and directories such as telephone directories and indexes of theses;
● non-academic publications such as newspapers, magazines, comics, newsletters, circulars, journals and biographies;
● financial records such as company accounts, sales figures, taxation records, and investment records;
● ephemera such as memoranda, internal notes, position papers, lists of recommendations, and household bills.

Such a list of classifications is not exhaustive, but at least gives a picture of the wide range of documents which are available. In addition, all of these exist in their own right anyway, and are not created specifically for the purpose of research.

It may be helpful to consider some of the above types of documents, and the ways in which they can be used in case-study research. When conducting a case study of an organisation or company, for example, it is often very informative to evaluate the marketing and official literature produced by that organisation. Such literature will frequently provide details of the products of the organisation, of its corporate structure and staffing, of its profit and export levels, and of possible proposed future developments and expansion. Most importantly, there will often be a form of corporate-mission statement, which sets out the goals and general philosophy of the organisation. This is very interesting from a researcher's viewpoint, because it will reflect the perspective and world view of the senior managers of the organisation. As the case study develops, it should be possible to check the congruency of this viewpoint with those of the people working within the organisation.

The telephone directory may not at first seem a very promising source of research data, but in fact it is widely used for research in for example, the distribution of surnames. A wide range of social and historical factors have been instrumental in affecting the distribution of people, and a study of surnames and their geographical location can shed light on some of these social influences. Comics and other light-entertainment publications can be very useful sources of data regarding social attitudes. They frequently reflect the values of popular culture, and can also provide a sequential record of changes in the norms of society.

In the early stages of examining a document, it is important to be as objective as possible about the quality of the information that it contains. In critically examining a document, it is important to ask several questions about it. The first thing that you should try to discover is the writer of the document; this may shed some light on the background to the document, and also on any possible bias which may have been in operation during its production. The document may reflect only a partial view, because of the specific interests of the writer. It may be possible to corroborate suppositions about the writer if other evidence is available.

Another important question is the reason why the document was produced. It may have been requested by an official body, and in such an instance it would be interesting to know the degree of that organisation's influence. The document might be part of a much larger study or review. On the other hand, it may have been produced solely for the interest of the writer.

Other critical questions include the place and date of the document's production. Both of these pieces of information are crucial in positioning the document within some kind of social and historical context. The key questions thus become 'Who? Why? Where? and When?'

Finally, it is extremely useful to know if there are any other similar documents in existence, whether or not by the author of the specific document being examined. These can help to verify the content of the document.

Documents have a number of advantages and disadvantages as data, and these are summarised in Figure 8.1.

Advantages

- Many types of document are easy to obtain because they already exist in the public domain, and using them may result in considerable savings in time and effort for the researcher when compared with the problems of collecting the equivalent data oneself.
- Unlike many other kinds of data collection, the researcher does not risk altering data by intruding upon a natural setting.
- Documents are very useful for studying cases in which elements of human discourse or activity are regarded as being private.

Disadvantages

- The document has not been produced for the purpose of the case study, and may not therefore generate precisely the kind of data which is required.
- Documents may not produce a continuous account because they reflect a situation at a specific time.
- Interpretation and analysis may be difficult because of the uncertain origin of the document.

Figure 8.1 The advantages and disadvantages of documents as data

The first disadvantage noted in Figure 8.1 can create difficulties when analysing documents for a case study. You may have identified several key issues to investigate within a case study, and you may be examining documents in order to develop these issues further. A single document, however, may only hint at one possible line of enquiry, or may suggest the development of a single theoretical idea. Other documents may supplement this idea, or may indeed set you off in an entirely different direction. The problem is that the documents are not part of a planned research investigation, and thus cannot be expected to provide data in a systematic order. In a sense, you have to take what you are given, and put the data into the best order you can.

Maintaining objectivity

One may try to think of objectivity in an absolute sense, as if it were feasible to design a research study which eliminated any possible effects or influence on the part of the researcher. According to such a view, the research would be designed to permit no interaction with the researcher, and the data analysis would proceed in such a way that the viewpoint of the researcher would have no impact at all. There is a tendency to think of scientific research in a laboratory as proceeding in this manner, but whether or not this is actually the case is a complex question.

However, case-study investigations rarely set out to achieve this kind of objectivity. There is a rather different concept of objectivity, which is concerned more with making public the grounds upon which one believes something to be true. This is a much more relevant concept of objectivity for the case study. What we are saying here, is that while we cannot totally eliminate our own viewpoints and preconceptions from the data analysis, we can at least try to document the nature of our particular world view, so that people reading the research can build this into their own interpretation of the account. This notion of objectivity seeks to acknowledge the fact that elements of subjectivity are inevitable in research, and particularly in qualitative research, but that we can reduce the effects by trying to be as analytical as possible about the interaction between ourselves and the research process.

An important criterion by which to judge case-study research is that of internal validity. This is concerned with the extent to which the data that has been collected can genuinely be regarded as being a reflection of the real state of the world. For example, when you are interviewing a person in order to collect information for a case study the person may not reveal their true feelings, or may only give you a partial picture of the situation; this may happen for a variety of reasons. In addition, the interviewee may not have really formulated a personal viewpoint on a particular subject, but may feel that an opinion has to be given for the sake of the interview. In such cases, the internal validity of the data will be much reduced. Another example is when you are making observations on a particular setting, and are writing up your field notes. Suppose you are writing a case study of a single secondary school. While you are visiting one day, you observe an unruly crowd of pupils, and conclude that this reflects the standard of behaviour in the school. It later transpires that these pupils were among a group from a neighbouring school who were visiting at the time. In other words, things were not as they seemed to be. The data exhibited a low degree of internal validity.

It remains a truism, but one which is worth noting, that data and the phenomenon represented by that data are not the same thing. The crowd of unruly pupils and the field notes resulting from the observation are different; the latter is merely a reflection of the former. The researcher is an intermediary between the data and the event; the researcher interprets the event and filters it through their consciousness. The resulting data is in many ways a reflection of the interpretive work carried out by the researcher. Thus we can begin to see that questions of internal validity lead us into complex philosophical problems concerning the reality of the external world and the way in which observers seek firstly to internalise that reality, and then to describe it for the consumption of others.

Questions of external validity are rather different but equally complex. External validity is concerned with the extent to which the results of one case study can be applied to other situations. Critics of case studies usually argue that the approach has limited usefulness because it is difficult, if not impossible, to generalise the results to other situations. On the other hand, advocates of the case-study approach would probably suggest that the question of generalisability is an inappropriate one in the first place. In addressing this question Yin (1989, p.21; see the 'Further reading' section) has argued the following:

> However, consider for the moment that the same question had been asked about an experiment . . . In fact, scientific facts are rarely based on single experiments; they are usually based on a multiple set of experiments, which have replicated the same phenomenon under different conditions.

If we accept Yin's viewpoint, then it is probably rather unfair to suggest that a case study is limited in value because it is impossible to generalise from the results. In a sense, case studies are not designed for generalisation. They are a totally different approach to research when compared with the survey, for example. The case study sets out to explore one particular situation in great depth, and is usually characterised by a richness and complexity of data which is never attained with, say, survey research.

This is not to say that one cannot generalise from a single case study, but that generalisation is qualitatively different from the situation with a survey. Statistical generalisation is clearly out of the question with a case study. However, the reader of a case-study report may well find that the picture portrayed strikes a chord with their personal experience of similar situations. If this is so, then there is an element of practical generalisation here. Another approach is to take up the point made by Yin above, and to conduct a range of case studies, each designed to explore issues raised in the previous one.

—— Action-research approaches ——

'Action research' is not a term which need necessarily be associated with a case-study approach, although the two concepts fit well together, and there is a convenience in looking at them simultaneously. It is not easy to produce a short, precise definition of action research, and in some ways it is easier to discuss the range of the term's application. However, it may be helpful to start with a contemporary definition made by Hopkins (1993, p.44; see the 'Further reading' section):

> Action research combines a substantive act with a research procedure; it is action disciplined by enquiry, a personal attempt at understanding while engaged in a process of improvement and reform.

This is a very good starting point from which we can now examine the way in which action research is applied. First of all, action research almost inevitably takes place in a 'real-life', practical setting such as a workplace. The reason for this is that the whole approach is designed to explore the impact of change upon practical situations. In order for action research to be relevant, there must be a practical context in which an element of change can be introduced. The change is introduced through 'action', from which the term 'action research' is derived.

It follows that action research is frequently initiated by individuals who are participants in the practical situation. These are people who are 'insiders', and who know the intimate workings of the organisation or the workplace. They can recognise contexts in which it might be possible to achieve improvements by initiating change. This is not to say that action research cannot be conducted by 'outsiders', but they may be in a more difficult position when it comes to introducing change. They may, however, be able to work with those within the organisation in a collaborative research team. This can often be a useful approach for case-study action research, because when a change is introduced, the ramifications can often be extensive, and a team of people may be necessary to monitor and map the consequences.

Action research starts with the identification of an area within an organisation or workplace setting, in which change could be introduced, and where there is the possibility that such change might be beneficial. The researcher then introduces the change, and monitors the consequences. Action research is not, however, necessarily intended to operate as a limited investigation of change; the nature of the feedback from the 'action' can be used to determine future priorities. The purpose of such action research is always to improve the research issue in question, thus action research is not a matter of research for its own sake, but more of wishing to learn from an investigation, and to make progress for the future.

Action research also has benefits for the researcher, which is one of the key features of this approach. The purpose is to encourage the researcher to engage in introspective reflection on an issue, and to examine the way in which interaction can take place between the researcher and the research issue. The action-research approach can help people to have a much more positive and interesting engagement with their work context.

The approach could be very useful for case studies conducted while students are on work placements. It is usually necessary for students to write up a report of what they have learned, which could easily be supplemented by a piece of action research. Suppose, for example, that you are working in a large organisation and wish to explore how suggestions from the workforce are treated by middle management. You could start by making a very minor suggestion in a friendly and helpful manner, and then observe the way in which it is treated. Depending upon the result, you might try again, and could approach the research issue in a slightly different way. The outcome of this action research would be a case study of the way in which a large organisation treats suggestions from the staff. Action research and case studies are thus not necessarily connected, although much action research could very easily be regarded as a study of a particular case.

Summary

To summarise, researchers employ case studies because:

- they provide an in-depth picture of a situation;
- they can use a variety of data;
- the process of data collection is often very interesting.

NEW CONCEPTS	
Category	Participant observation

9

INTERVIEW RESEARCH

Types of interview

The interview is one of the most commonly used techniques for collecting data. It has many advantages as a research method. The interview is reasonably straightforward to organise, and as a process is understood by potential respondents; the latter have a fairly good idea of what is being asked of them. There is no extensive documentation to prepare prior to the interview, and in many cases detailed questions do not have to be thought out in advance by the researcher. The interview process also produces a great deal of data, and although this can sometimes pose problems of data management, it is often helpful to have a lot of available data. Taking part in a research interview is also often a very interesting experience, both for the interviewer and the interviewee. For the interviewer there is the opportunity to learn about someone else's thoughts, attitudes and aspirations, whereas for the interviewee it is often pleasant to have someone listening attentively to what you say, and showing interest in what you think about the world.

One of the most significant aspects of the interview is that it produces data of a detail and richness which it is difficult to acquire in any other way. When interviewees are feeling confident and relaxed they will often talk about and analyse their own thoughts in a detail which other research methods do not encourage. At the same time, it is important that there are safeguards in place to reassure interviewees that any information revealed will only be used for the specific, stated purposes agreed at the beginning of the interview.

Naturally there are also several disadvantages with the interview. The process is quite time-consuming when compared to, say, postal questionnaires. The interview cannot be rushed, and time must be taken to talk to the interviewee both before and after the actual interview. Partly because of this time factor, it is difficult to interview a large research sample, and this may affect the degree of generalisation which it is possible to draw from the data.

The research interview can be approached in a variety of different ways. It is possible to use the interview approach in conjunction with a detailed schedule of questions in order to conduct a survey. In this case, the questions are likely to be focused, and to require relatively brief responses. On the other hand, the researcher can plan in advance a series of topics to be discussed during an interview, yet leave the interviewee considerable freedom to talk about whatever they want to, within this broad framework. Finally, the researcher can make very few plans prior to the interview, simply agreeing a general topic and then allowing the interviewee to control the direction of the discussion.

Interviews vary enormously, then, in terms of both the extent of the preplanning of questions, and of the degree of control which the interviewer seeks to exercise over the research process. There may be a careful planning of questions, or simply an agreement about a general discussion topic. The researcher may wish to control the content and pace of the interview, or may prefer to encourage the interviewee to guide its format. There are both advantages and disadvantages with different interview models, and in addition there are methodological assumptions about the type of data and knowledge revealed by differing approaches. These will now be discussed in the following sections.

——— Planning the interview ———

If interviews are to proceed smoothly and effectively, and are also to be a pleasant experience for interviewer and interviewee, then they must be carefully planned. As Anderson (1990, p.222; see the 'Further reading' section) writes:

> We use interviews in all walks of life for a wide range of purposes and to use it for research purposes requires more care and skill than is commonly exercised.

The location for the interview is an early consideration, and is to some extent influenced by the proposed nature of the interview. For example, if it is intended to interview construction workers about health and safety issues, then it is important to decide on a time and location during the working day when the workers will be available for interview. A preliminary visit to the construction site may be necessary in order to establish a time when the workers are relaxed, and are normally available to talk on a one-to-one basis. The mid-morning break may be a possibility, and it may be decided to engage the workers in informal conversation as they sit drinking their morning coffee. In this environment interviews will inevitably be informal, and notes may have to be written after the event.

In a large, formal organisation, the situation will be very different. It may be possible to reserve a room specifically for the interview. If there is a choice of rooms, then there are certain considerations which should be taken into account. People working within the organisation may not wish it to be too obvious that they are taking part in the interviews, and a fairly private room on a quiet corridor may therefore be preferable. It should be definitely booked for the duration of the interviews, as it is disconcerting for both the interviewer and interviewee to be interrupted. If both men and women are likely to be involved in the interviews, then it may be preferable to have a room with a glass window set in the door. This may help to set both parties at their ease. The room should be comfortable, with a table on which participants can place their documents. Care should be taken that chairs are at the same height; if, for example, the interviewee is sitting in a much lower chair than the interviewer, this may enhance any feelings of differential status or power. If it is intended to use a tape recorder during the interview, then it may be helpful if a convenient electrical socket, and also a discrete location for the recorder, are available. This is not to say that the recorder should be hidden, but it may be better to locate it on one side of the room and not, for example, directly between the interviewer and the interviewee. If you wish to use a tape recorder, it is clearly important to seek the permission of the interviewee first.

As with all research, but perhaps particularly with the interview, it is a good idea to brief the potential respondent carefully before the data-gathering commences. The interview is a particularly personal encounter, and the respondent may have a number of concerns about the research process. Among the questions which might come into the respondent's mind are the following:

- Will I be quoted on what I say?
- Which other people might they talk to about what I say?
- If I say something I regret, can I take it back?
- If I feel things have gone a bit too far, how can I stop the interview?
- What will they use the interview for?

These are legitimate questions, and it is only fair to try to provide clear answers before respondents commit themselves to the interview. One way in which to provide clear and consistent answers is to give all the possible respondents a letter prior to the interview, which explains everything that they might wish to know. Such a letter might read like this:

Dear . . .

I should be very grateful if you would be able to take part in a research project which I am organising to investigate the attitudes of parents to discipline in schools. I hope to interview a number of parents about this topic. The research is part of a project connected with the local university.

Each interview will last about 15 minutes. Your comments will be used to write a research report which is likely to be published. Your name will not be used, nor will any reference be made to your child, or children, or to the school(s) attended.

During the actual interview, please feel free to end the interview at any time, or to take back a comment that you would like to rephrase. If you agree, I would like to tape record the interview because it gives me an accurate record of it. All tapes will be recorded over once the research is written up. However, if you prefer, I will make notes during the interview, rather than use a tape recorder.

Any information that you are able to give will be very important to us in our efforts to help schools to provide the kind of environment that parents want for their children. We hope that you will be able to take part.

Yours sincerely

The advantage of a letter such as this is that, once prepared, it can easily be distributed to a great many people. Equally, all the recipients of the letter are given the same standard information. They are able, if they so wish, to refuse to take part in the interviews, and the letter gives them the chance to think it over. Careful preparation such as this should reassure respondents, and should help to create a pleasant atmosphere during the actual interview.

--------- # The interview process ---------

A good way in which to start the interview is to refer to the letter which you used to enlist the help of interviewees. You could ask if there are any questions arising from the letter, or issues which the respondent wishes to clarify.

If you intend to use a tape recorder, then you can perhaps enquire again whether the interviewee agrees to this. It may be reassuring to the interviewee if the tape recorder is placed within reach, and if you indicate the stop/start control. You can invite them to stop the recorder if they begin to feel unhappy about its use. This sense of control may give the respondent a much greater feeling of ease.

In terms of questioning, it is best to begin with a very general, open-ended question. For example, in an interview study of the work role of hotel receptionists, you could start with a question such as:

Well, tell me what it is like to be a hotel receptionist;

or

The job sounds very varied to me. What kinds of things do you have to do?

or

You must have to deal with lots of different people. What is that like?

Such questions are designed to encourage the interviewee to talk, without having any specific focus to the discussion. Once the interviewee appears to be slowing down, in terms of what is being said, then the interviewer can select one aspect of their response and ask a more focused question. By asking more and more focused questions, eventually the line of questioning will be exhausted, and the interviewer can once again revert to a more general question. This is assuming that an **interview schedule**, which lists a precise order of questions, is not used.

Care must be taken when phrasing questions, and much of what has already been said regarding survey techniques is also relevant here. It is important to ensure that you avoid the use of inappropriate pronouns in terms of gender. For example one might ask a question such as:

How does the manager react when he finds that sales are down?

There is no need to assume that the manager is male rather than female, unless this has been referred to earlier. It is just as easy to say:

How does the manager react when sales are down?

In a research interview it is undesirable to challenge the opinions of an interviewee, or to be confrontational in other ways. The respondent is offering their time and energy to help with the research, and it seems very unfair to challenge what is being said. The purpose of research is primarily accurately to record what is being said, and to analyse it as data; it is not meant to show the personal preferences of the interviewer.

In general, it is a good idea for the interviewer to try to create a pleasant atmosphere in which the interviewee can enjoy the conversation. If this is the case, then not only may the interviewee give a positive impression of the research to others, but they may also provide more detailed responses, and hence richer data.

It is important for the researcher to have an idea of the intended duration of the interview, and to make this clear to the respondent in advance. The interviewee then knows what to expect, and can make the appropriate personal arrangements. Having given such an undertaking in terms of the interview's duration, the researcher should try to stick to the time schedule. When the time for ending the interview is approaching, the researcher should begin to indicate this, using a strategy such as the following:

Well, that is very interesting. Is there anything you want to add to this discussion?
All right, well thank you very much for your help – what you have said has certainly made me think about this issue.
Before we finish, are there any questions that you would like to ask me?
Well, thank you very much for your help. It is much appreciated.

This helps to create a clear and unambiguous end to the interview, and assists the researcher in staying on schedule for future interviews.

Recording data

There are probably two main aspects to consider regarding the recording of interview data. Firstly, there is the actual method itself and, secondly, the impact which this may have on the interviewee. Some methods are more intrusive than others.

Perhaps the least intrusive method is simply to conduct the interview as a conversation, and then to write up your notes immediately afterwards. This has the least possible impact upon the interviewee, but clearly raises questions about the accuracy of the data. The note-taking can, of course, be done during the interview. It may be possible, for example, to write down key words or utterances, and to use these to prepare more detailed notes afterwards. A shorthand facility will obviously help here. Taking notes while talking to someone can, however, be distracting for the interviewee, and also difficult for the interviewer.

The alternative is to use an audio- or videotape recorder. This may, or may not, be regarded as intrusive, depending upon the attitude of the interviewee. Some people may feel very nervous when confronted with a tape recorder, while others may remain unaffected. Certainly this method produces the most accurate data. The video recorder has the advantage that it also records facial expressions, gestures and other non-verbal forms of communication during the interview; these can be later analysed as supplementary data to the spoken word.

After the interview, it is normal to transcribe the tape into written form. It can be written out rather like a play script, giving the names (real or invented) of the participants. The written version can then be analysed.

In writing up research, it is usual to select extracts or quotations from the interview transcripts to use for supplementary arguments, or for illustrative purposes.

The interview schedule

In its formal sense, an interview schedule consists of a detailed plan for the conduct of an interview. It contains instructions for the interviewer, an introduction which should be read to each respondent, and a series of questions arranged in a specific sequence, which is not varied for different respondents. The schedule may be arranged like a form, with boxes within which to code the responses, and there may also be questions for the interviewer to complete about, say, the date and time of the interview.

Other interview schedules may vary enormously. They may consist simply of a list of questions designed as reminders to the interviewer, or perhaps of a few topics which the interviewer hopes to explore. Whatever their format, they serve to act as a prompt for the interviewer and, if required, to ensure a degree of consistency in the interviews with different people.

Whether or not a schedule is necessary depends upon the particular philosophical approach to the interview. In the case of a completely **unstructured interview**, a schedule is not required, because the interviewee controls the pace and content of the interview. No consistency between interviews is intended. However, if it is intended to encourage interviewees to respond to the same questions or issues, then some form of schedule is most desirable.

During the interview, it is probably best to use the schedule as unobtrusively as possible. If it is used to read from, for example, it can make the interview appear extremely formal. The interviewer should memorise its questions and topics as far as possible, and should refer to the schedule only as a prompt.

Structured interviews

In some ways, separating interview strategies into those that are 'structured' and those that are 'unstructured' is a rather artificial distinction. It is more accurate to regard the different forms of interviews as existing on a continuum from being highly structured, to being deliberately unstructured by the researcher. Nevertheless, those interviews in which the researcher has predetermined the preferred structure do have certain characteristics which distinguish them from the unstructured interview.

In the **structured interview**, the researcher deliberately tries to retain considerable control over the content of the conversation. The researcher has usually identified some topics or questions which he or she has defined as being central to the broad purpose of the interview. This process of definition can be both an advantage and a disadvantage: while it ensures some degree of consistency in the different interviews, it tends to impose the researcher's view of events upon the respondents. The researcher analyses the topic which is the subject of the research project, and then formulates questions which are defined as being the most significant on those issues. However, it is almost impossible to conceive of a single researcher who is familiar with all the relevant issues in a research project, and consequently this approach may result in new data being missed. Unless respondents are given an opportunity to present their unique and individual view of events they may simply use the framework provided by the researcher. This approach may leave some of the interviewees wishing that they had more of an opportunity to provide their own interpretations of the research topic.

Structured interviews normally employ some kind of interview schedule, which provides consistency to the data collection. This general consistency is also reflected in a normally preplanned length for the interview. Determining the approximate duration of the interview also ensures a consistency in the approximate amount of time devoted to a particular question.

—— Unstructured interviews ——

An unstructured interview is unstructured in the sense that the interviewer does not attempt to plan a sequence and pattern for the discussion. This does not mean that the interviewer has absolutely no agenda for the interview, but rather that the interview is likely to be very informal, and that the interviewer will invite the interviewee to lead the discussion in new directions. As Sanger (1996, p.63; see the 'Further reading' section) writes:

> In principle, it allows all parties to participate in the generation of an agenda and permits the interviewee to be proactive in that process.

The interviewer deliberately relinquishes control of the process, and encourages interviewees to provide their own definition of events. The process recognises that during an interview the participants frequently meet within a sphere of multiple realities, and that no single interpretation is likely to point to the 'truth'.

In order to encourage the interviewee's participation, the interviewer will usually ask open-ended questions, which leave the interviewee considerable freedom to direct the discussion. The interviewer will often take a lead from the interviewee, and will allow the discussion to develop according to the latter's apparent wishes. There is usually no requirement for an interview schedule. The interviewer may have in mind several topics to raise during the discussion, but this provisional plan will probably be adapted in the light of the evolving conversation. Equally, the interview may have no predetermined length, but will continue for as long as the participants wish.

Unstructured interviews are very useful for situations in which the researcher knows relatively little about the topic being investigated, and wishes to build up a picture of the relevant research issues. The comments made by the respondents can be used to construct a plan of the interrelationships between research issues, which can then be used to develop more precise investigations.

On the other hand, unstructured interviews are much used as a research technique in their own right, for those occasions when the chosen research perspective requires a definition of reality by the respondent. This type of interview can then become the substantive data-collection method for the research.

The elite interview

One type of interview which may be either structured or unstructured, is the **elite interview**. This is a term given to an interview in which the respondent is an individual who has been specifically identified as being able to provide special insights into the research topic. The respondent is, in fact, a 'key respondent'. Such a respondent may possess:

- special knowledge or skills;
- experience of working within a particular organisation;
- a willingness to provide detailed information, and to participate in a series of lengthy interviews.

The respondent may be identified by the researcher either:

- by being mentioned in the media;
- by personal recommendation;
- by offering to participate as a research respondent.

Respondents may also be identified by the recommendation of previous key respondents.

Elite interviews can thus provide data which may be otherwise unavailable, because of the special knowledge and insights of a carefully selected group of respondents.

───────── Summary ─────────

In conclusion, researchers use interviews in their research design because:

- they are relatively easy to organise;
- they provide a great deal of rich, interesting data;
- they are generally enjoyable for the participants, both the researcher and the respondent;
- they can be adapted to the needs of different locations and situations;
- they can be used either as part of survey research, or of a variety of other research designs.

NEW CONCEPTS

Elite interview	Structured interview
Interview schedule	Unstructured interview

ANALYSING
YOUR DATA

10
QUALITATIVE DATA

Sorting the data

Probably the main characteristic of qualitative research is the very large amount of data which it generates. Nowhere is this better illustrated than with interview data. If you tape record an interview with someone, and then play the tape back, it may not seem very long; perhaps it lasts for 20 or 30 minutes. However, if you transcribe the tape, and thus turn it into something resembling a play script, it will not only take you a long time, but will produce a very long transcript indeed.

There is much the same situation with a field diary. If you keep notes about a case study for any period of time the notes quickly build up into a substantial document. Even a few notes made systematically every day accumulate into a large data source. Having a lot of data is in many ways very useful; it is certainly a better state of affairs than having insufficient data, but it also poses particular problems.

The first thing to do with qualitative data is to sort it into manageable sections. Up to a point, it is possible to sort qualitative data as it is being gathered. Suppose that while you are interviewing someone, you ask questions about a particular theme, and then file the responses to that theme once the interview is over. In this way you can build up files of data on particular issues, themes or questions. On the other hand, it is not very easy to do this at the beginning of a research study, because you do not necessarily know the themes in which you are interested. It often takes a good deal of preliminary research in order to suggest what some of these themes might be.

The early stages of qualitative research usually involve collecting any data that might be of interest or value to resolving the aims of the research project. In other words, one develops a kind of magpie approach. At this stage of the research it is not always easy to know what will be useful and what is superfluous. Let us start by looking at the stages of the sorting process, and let us imagine that our research project involves a mixture of interview data and documentary data.

The first stage is to get something of a feeling for the scope and depth of the data. Getting a grasp of the full content of qualitative data is often difficult; while we are involved in the actual process of data collection we nearly always remember some aspects of the data, but not in a very systematic way. We should first scan the data and begin to understand something of the content. During this process, something will almost certainly stick in your mind as being an interesting opinion expressed by a respondent, or as a perceptive comment on a research issue. Let us suppose that we are researching the attitudes of workers regarding their motivation and fulfilment at work. A brief look at the interview data may reveal that the idea of an 'interesting' job keeps cropping up. 'Interest' seems to be a crucial aspect for many of the respondents: they want, above all, a job which 'interests' them, although most do not define what they mean by 'interest' or 'interesting'. The first stage in the data-sorting process is therefore to take all the references to 'interest', and to file them together. This is not always easy to do, since these references and notes may be embedded within other data. One strategy is to cut out the references to a particular subject with scissors, and to place them all together, perhaps in a single file.

When the data was originally collected, you may also have noted the name of the particular respondent and the date, time and location of the interview. It will be necessary to copy this information onto the section which has been cut out. If you want to be really well organised, you might try producing a pro-forma record along the lines illustrated in Figure 10.1.

Once produced, this pro-forma record can be photocopied in large numbers. The data extract is glued onto it, and any relevant information about the source is added in the appropriate section. Indeed, in many ways it is more convenient to file a standard sheet like this on every occasion. The filing can be done by subject area, and within that category alphabetically by respondent surname. The other technique is to input the extracts of data into a computer, and then to use the 'sort' facilities which are now very common in wordprocessing packages.

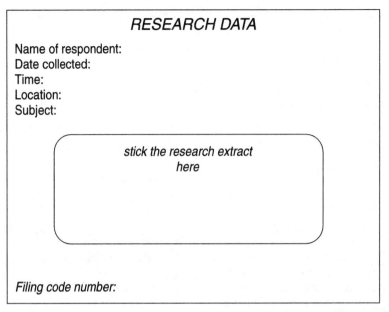

Figure 10.1 Example of a pro-forma record

As you cut out extracts from the original data, you should take care not to lose the sense of coherence within the remainder of the data. If you are using a computer, then one technique is to use a fluorescent highlighter pen on the hard copy to indicate the sections of text which have already been entered into the computer. This helps to ensure that data is not used twice to justify different viewpoints. A single piece of data can, of course, be interpreted in several different ways, and there is no reason why it should not be used in different categories. However, in this case it is important to record this by means of some form of crossreferencing system so that you do not forget that you have done so.

The process of sorting the data should continue until the vast majority of the significant data is placed into named categories. It is not always easy to place all of your data into a single category, and this is not necessarily a problem; data which is difficult to categorise can be set on one side until it is needed. At some stage in the future, new categories may be generated, and then this data may prove useful.

The sorting of qualitative data is a gradual, ongoing process. It should not be regarded as a process which, once accomplished, is fixed in stone. The purpose of this early sorting stage is to begin to make some sense of the sheer magnitude of data which has been assembled. The categories which have been developed are provisional; they are the best which can be done with the data at this point. The provisional categories are given names to indicate the main concept which appears to be common to all data within that category, and this key concept will be central to the developing analysis of the data.

At this stage, fragments of data have been placed in what seem to be the appropriate categories. However, it must be conceded that:

* the categories, along with their associated key concepts, may not be the most appropriate means of sorting the data in all cases;
* some categories may include other key concepts which have not yet been determined;
* some data may have been placed in more than one category. This is not necessarily a problem (and is discussed in more detail later);
* the process of categorising data is very much a subjective process. The researcher applies the most objective possible process to making sense of the data, while acknowledging that the analytical decisions made are inevitably affected by the individual researcher's perspective;
* the names which are given to key concepts may be the ones chosen by respondents, or may be concepts which are superimposed by the researcher upon the data. Either approach may be used, but it is important to acknowledge the process which is being adopted.

We will now examine in more detail the actual process of coding data.

Post-coding the data

When developing a data-collection instrument for qualitative research, there is usually very little systematic attempt made to categorise the responses as they are being collected. This approach is the opposite taken in quantitative research, where data is usually automatically coded and categorised on collection. In a survey, for example, a questionnaire item may ask:

> **How would you rate your level of interest in your current employment duties?**
>
> 1 Very interesting and stimulating ——
> 2 Interesting for a good deal of the time ——
> 3 Interesting at times, but generally not very stimulating ——
> 4 Of very little interest value at all ——

In this case, the responses of the subject are pre-coded, and the subject has only four alternative responses. In qualitative research, the subject would more probably be asked a question such as:

What are your feelings about the interest value of your employment?

All kinds of data may emerge from the ensuing discussion, and it is necessary to superimpose some kind of structure upon that data. As indicated previously, the subject may use all kinds of concepts to express their feelings, and it is the job of the researcher to decide which are the most appropriate. The essential difference between **pre-coding** and **post-coding** is as follows:

- pre-coding: the categories and concepts are determined by the researcher;
- post-coding: the categories and concepts are suggested by the subject, and the researcher builds upon them.

An important difference in the philosophical and conceptual approaches to research is indicated here. In qualitative research, the researcher adopts what is, in effect, a much more interactive debate with the subjects of the research.

When respondents are providing data, they structure their view of the world in their own way; they impose their own analysis upon their experiences, and use their own words to express that analysis. Normally, a researcher would be happy to let that process continue, unless the respondent appeared to be having some difficulty in formulating a satisfactory analysis for themselves. The researcher might then intervene and make suggestions about how they might organise their ideas. At this stage, however, the researcher would have to use ideas which had some meaning and significance for the subjects; it would be unsatisfactory to employ complex academic concepts which had little meaning for the respondents.

However, it is very important for the qualitative researcher to acknowledge either whether the post-coding categories have come primarily from the subjects, or whether they have been mainly suggested by the researcher; each involves a basic difference of approach. If the respondent's coding concepts are being used, then it is the respondent's view of the world which is being incorporated into the research; if the researcher's concepts are being used, then a different approach must be acknowledged. This is not to suggest that one approach is correct and the other wrong – only that it should be clear to the reader of the research that a particular kind of approach has been adopted.

Developing categories

The processes of post-coding the data and of developing conceptual categories merge together. Analysing qualitative data is not a process which can easily be subdivided into sections; it is rather more a continuum which exists throughout the research process – while the data is being collected and also, of course, afterwards. In addition, it is a process which is often difficult to exclude from one's mind; even during everyday activities, new ideas for analysis come to mind, and are best jotted down immediately as an *aide-mémoire*, as those ideas may not recur.

However, as mentioned earlier, there are two issues involved in category formation which it is important to acknowledge, and these are that:

- the same data may be used in the development of more than one category;
- it must be acknowledged that the process of categorisation is a very subjective process, whether it is done by the researcher or by the respondent.

In the case of the same data being used to substantiate more than one category, consider the case of an investigation into the relative importance of course fees and of course content in determining whether a student will enrol at a specific college or university. It may transpire in discussions with students that both issues are important, but that one can outweigh the other, depending upon the circumstances prevalent at the time. Such interview data can therefore be used to support the idea of a category of 'course cost', or of a category of 'course content'. The researcher will have to make a subjective decision regarding the balance of emphasis of the data: does it in general place emphasis upon cost, or upon content? The data will have to be used according to the apparent emphasis. When there is great difficulty in making a decision, the data could be used to support both categories, but in such a case it is important to make clear the basis of such a decision, and to locate the decision-making process firmly in the public realm.

This takes us on to the issue of the subjectivity of decision-making. With qualitative data, it is often possible to draw a number of different conclusions from the information given, according to the interpretation placed upon the data. This process is very subjective, and depends upon the nature of the analysis carried out by the individual researcher or respondent. We have only to think of the way in which this type of process occurs in everyday life. When two people are talking, for example, it is easy for one to misunderstand, or to misinterpret the other and, indeed, for offence to be taken. Usually such misunderstandings revolve around the misinterpretation of a non-verbal or verbal signal, and result from the carrying out of insufficient questioning work to establish the intended meaning.

If we are unclear about someone's intended meaning, we usually seek to clarify what was said. In the case of interview or observational data, however, we are not normally able to revisit the subject to confirm the meaning. The confirmation must therefore be carried out at the time. However, very often we think that we understand someone initially, only to discover later that we are unsure. By this time, we simply have to take an interpretive decision, and make the best use that we can of the data. The way in which we carry out this interpretive work is likely to depend upon our:

- academic background and training; the courses and disciplines that we have studied;
- research expertise and experience; specifically our background in methodology and data analysis;
- knowledge of the subject background of the data;
- familiarity with qualitative analysis.

—————————— **Grounded theory** ——————————

One of the main purposes for carrying out the type of category-forming described previously is to produce a theory. This is a general statement which links together two or more concepts or ideas, and which indicates how one concept affects the other. In addition, the theory should be capable of being practically tested by the collection of empirical evidence.

It could be argued that the production of a theory is the ultimate purpose of research. A good theory enables the researcher to provide a clear description of events, and of the categories, concepts and variables which are contributors to those events. The theory also enables future aspects of the situation to be accurately predicted when the understanding of the relationship between the variables is sufficiently accurate to enable their future connection to be accurately estimated. The other main function of a theory is to explain social events. In other words, a good theory should be able to explain the reasons why the variables interact and affect each other.

Glaser and Strauss (1967; see the 'Further reading' section) argued that the most appropriate way in which to generate such a theory was to base, or 'ground', it in the data being studied. The categories which are developed from the data are used to construct the theory, and the latter is very much part of the data. In fact, the process of theory construction does not wait until all data has been collected, but is rather an integral part of the process of data collection. The provisional, developing theory suggests fresh types of data which may be collected. This data helps in the revision and restructuring of the theory, which then possibly indicates a new line of enquiry. Theory, according to this model, is seen as continually developing and adapting to meet the requirements of the data. In other words, the theory has emerged from, and is an almost inseparable part of, the research data.

It can be argued that theory which is grounded in the data presents a better model of the world, and enables people to relate to it much better than is the case with a more abstract theory. **Grounded theory** may present a picture of data which is more immediate and 'real', and which is of greater relevance to the researcher.

One of the major contributions of the grounded-theory approach is the stress that it places upon the value of generating a theory, even if it only relates to a relatively narrow field or situation. The traditional approach to theory has been to try to work within the parameters set by some of the large-scale, social-science theorists, and to adapt these to the needs of the particular research being conducted. However, an alternative approach, and that advocated by the grounded-theory perspective, is to take every opportunity to build up a theory when this seems relevant and appropriate to the data. The emphasis, then, is upon the generation of the theory rather than on the process of continually trying to demonstrate the validity of the theory. According to this view, a theory is not seen as a finite construct which is able to explain the world, both now and in the future; rather it is viewed as an organic entity which grows, evolves and changes as it adapts to new data and circumstances.

Finally, in the grounded theory approach, research design, data collection and theorising are seen as simultaneous activities. They are not viewed as a temporal sequence, but rather as activities which inform and relate to each other, and which are equally and mutually important to each other.

—— Using computer packages ——

Traditionally, computers have been used to help the researcher to analyse quantitative data, but there have been many recent advances in computer applications with regard to qualitative data. The qualitative researcher normally collects a large volume of written or transcribed data, and then codes and categorises the material according to criteria which might be externally produced, or which might alternatively have developed from the data. The conduct of these tasks has typically involved low-technology techniques, such as the use of highlighting pens, index cards, cutting and pasting, and different filing strategies. As discussed previously, this process of categorisation can then lead on to theory building.

The main role of the computer in qualitative data analysis is to help with the mechanical aspects of data management. That is, the computer can make the processes of data sorting, coding, and retrieval much easier. In principle, it should be possible to handle large amounts of data using a computer, and also quickly to identify a particular piece of text in which the researcher is interested. The essential processes of analysis and theory construction are thus left in the hands of the researcher, while routine tasks are handled more speedily.

Computers can be used to identify the location of a specific word, or its variants. The number of times that a word occurs can be counted, and computer programs can also identify words that are related in meaning to the original word searched for. Some **software** can provide the researcher with information on the locations of a specific word throughout the text, indicating in which selected section the word can be found, or alternatively locating the word line by line.

Many types of software enable sections of data to be coded. For example, a group of sentences which have an interconnected meaning can be clustered together and given a code; other sentences can be similarly coded. The computer can then retrieve all the sections which are coded in the same way. Some sections can be coded with two separate codes, and some software will search for, and retrieve, those sections which are thus coded.

There appear to be a number of interesting computer applications which are likely to become more widely available in the future. One of the most time-consuming aspects of qualitative research has been the transcription of both field notes and interview tapes. It is now possible to speak into a microphone, and for the text to appear directly on the computer screen, ready to be 'saved' and be printed out. When this technology becomes more widely available, it will be possible to conduct an interview, and for the text to be printed out moments later. While this will have major advantages in terms of saving time, it is difficult to predict all of its consequences. The nature of the data-collection process can easily affect the data produced, and it is too early at the moment to predict the effects of future increasingly sophisticated research instruments.

A range of software is currently available which performs a variety of tasks, ranging from simple classification of text, to aspects of theory building. The software functions do overlap to some extent, and it is best to look carefully at a range of software before committing yourself to any. Weitzman and Miles (1995; see the 'Further reading' section) provide a thorough survey of the currently available software.

NEW CONCEPTS

Grounded theory	Pre-coding
Post-coding	Software

11
QUANTITATIVE DATA

Pre-coded data

When you pre-code data, you decide in advance of the data-collection process the categories and questions which you think will be significant in the research. You may base these assumptions upon a good deal of preliminary research, or alternatively they may simply represent briefly considered hunches. Nevertheless, this approach is rather different to the post-coding of qualitative research, whose categories tend to derive much more from the data itself, rather than from the preconceptions of the researcher.

The pre-coding of data can be seen as part of a general perspective shared with natural sciences such as physics and chemistry. The perspective of these subjects is that there are measurable entities in the world, which the scientist can quantify by using the appropriate measuring instruments. The social scientist who devises a social experiment, or who administers a precisely constructed questionnaire, is following in the same tradition. There are several important implications inherent in the notion of pre-coding data.

Firstly, the researcher is assumed to have an overview of the research problem, which is sufficiently comprehensive to enable them to define the most important issues which require further investigation. These then become the subjects for questionnaire items, interview questions, or key variables in an experimental design.

Secondly, the identified issues are regarded as being precisely measurable, and normally quantifiable. There is an assumption here about the nature of social phenomena: in allocating individuals to a particular social class, for instance, the researcher is assuming that 'social class' is a coherent concept with certain characteristics. Furthermore, there is the concept that social class exists at a number of different levels, and that individuals can be assigned to these levels. Not only are important philosophical questions being raised here concerning the quantitative measurement of such concepts, but also concerning the reality of social classifications. Even if you, as a researcher, allocate individuals to a particular social class, can you be sure that they accept this categorisation? No matter what the researcher thinks, is this categorisation reflected in reality? Is it simply a construct of the researcher? We may, for example, ask individuals whether they feel that they belong to a social class, and be told that they consider themselves 'classless', and that the concept of social class is, in their view, outmoded and irrelevant.

Thirdly, there is the concern that through this perspective of pre-coding respondents are very much restricted in what they can offer to the research process. The respondents may want the researcher to consider their interpretations and classifications of data. They may feel that they are the providers of the data, and therefore that they understand it better; they may feel that the pre-coding of data does not allow them to contribute their own ways of making sense of the data.

Pre-coding has many advantages, but it should be ensured that the researcher has a general background knowledge of the research area so that they can formulate the relevant codes and questions in advance. It is very difficult to negate the reservations expressed above, particularly the argument that pre-coding of necessity involves definitions by the researcher about the nature of the phenomena being investigated. Such features are an inevitable part of pre-coded data, and should be accepted along with the advantages, which can be summarised as:

- a certainty that different respondents will be presented with questions in a uniform format;
- the facility to structure questions in such a form that the responses are appropriately arranged for statistical analysis;
- the facility to introduce quantification where necessary;
- control by the researcher over all the aspects of research design.

Pre-coding is thus intrinsically different from post-coding as a methodological approach. Rather than thinking of some aspects of pre-coding as advantages and others as disadvantages, it may be more helpful simply to regard them as features of a particular approach to research. To some extent, this then removes us from a confrontational debate about the best research approach. We in effect accept that there are a variety of research approaches and perspectives, all of which are relevant to different research problems. Rather than having a preferred methodology, we thus select the approach which seems the most suitable for the research issue being addressed.

—— The basis of statistical analysis ——

Statistics are important in the analysis of quantitative data in a number of ways, for example:

- they enable us to judge whether a hypothesis can be reasonably supported by the evidence;
- they help us to assess the extent to which results from a sample may be generalised to a wider population.

We can rarely collect data from an entire population, and so must rely on a sample instead, but want to know how confident we can be in generalising from the results of the sample to the rest of the universe.

Statistical techniques are a set of mathematical procedures which enable us to resolve some of these issues as accurately as we can. They provide us with answers within certain limits of accuracy. The word 'statistics' can therefore be used to describe the mathematical procedures which are used either to describe social situations, or to draw inferences from them, but they can also be used in giving the numerical results of statistical analysis. The word is perhaps also more loosely used for any numerical array of data.

Statistics have a very wide application in many subject areas. There are, however, two main types of statistical approaches. The first is termed **descriptive statistics**, and involves the collection and summarisation of numerical information about a topic. The data can be analysed to determine certain key features in terms of, say, the most common figures or changes which have taken place from previous years. A supermarket, for example, might be interested in knowing how much is spent in each section of its store, and also the amount spent by each customer in each separate section. Using a computer program, it would be quite easy to identify these figures using the product codes registered at the checkout. Such figures could be used to calculate, for example, the average amount spent by each customer in different supermarket sections.

The essence of descriptive statistics is that they present an array of numerical data, and then manipulate and analyse it in various ways in order to provide as comprehensive a picture as possible. They do not, however, attempt to explain the figures in terms of other changes and variables. There would be no attempt, for example, to try to explain sales figures in relation to, say, country-wide economic indicators; there would also be no attempt to predict future trends in sales figures. Such activities would be the province of **inferential statistics**.

A good example of the use of inferential statistics is in the work of actuaries in insurance companies. The actuary examines descriptive statistics, but then relates these to a variety of social variables in an attempt to predict future trends. An obvious example is the case of motor insurance: we can collect data on car accidents and then summarise these in various ways to make them more understandable. These summaries would then constitute descriptive statistics. On the other hand, we could relate the accidents to a particular variable, such as the age of the driver. The actuary calculates the probability that a person of a certain age will have a motor-car accident in the future. Such inferential statistical calculations enable insurance premiums to be calculated for drivers of different ages.

Inferential statistics are thus concerned with two main types of issue. Firstly, they enable an estimate to be made of the extent to which characteristics of a sample are true of the entire population being studied. This is a very important type of statistical inference because it is rarely possible for a researcher to collect data from all members of the population; as discussed earlier, a sample must instead be drawn. The second major function of inferential statistics is to establish the connection between variables. This often takes the form of testing hypotheses.

The data which is used in quantitative analysis is of several different kinds. The simplest type of data is termed **nominal data**, and this data is derived by placing individuals into named categories. There is no quantitative connection between the categories; they simply constitute named groupings. We might allocate people to groups based upon the county or state in which they reside; these categories would be nominal data. The second type of data (in increasing order of sophistication) is **ordinal data**. This type of data consists of values arranged in order of magnitude, but where the difference between the values is not known. For example, if we list the children of a school class in the order in which a teacher thinks the children have made an effort, then we will have ordinal data. The children are listed in rank order according to a particular criterion, but we do not know the extent of the difference between adjacent children in the list.

The next most sophisticated type of data is called **interval data**. A variable expressed as interval data has equal gaps between the individual measurements on the scale of values, but there is no meaningful zero level. The result is that it is possible to state the distance of each measurement from every other measurement, but it is not possible to divide one figure by another to obtain a ratio.

Temperature scales can be considered as being examples of interval data. In the case of temperatures expressed as either degrees centigrade or degrees Fahrenheit, it is understood by how much one temperature reading differs from another temperature reading. However, in both cases, 0° centigrade or Fahrenheit do not refer to temperatures in which there is a total absence of heat: they are temperatures chosen as being zero degrees from, in a sense, a purely arbitrary viewpoint. Indeed, it is possible to have temperatures that are much lower than zero degrees on both scales. The result of this is that 100°F is not twice as hot as 50°F, and similarly on the centigrade scale. If, however, we measure temperature from the theoretically absolute zero of 0° Kelvin, or approximately –273° centigrade, then we have a different type of scale. This kind of scale is called a ratio scale, and not only are its individual measurements the same space apart, but one figure can be compared to another, since they are both based upon the same, meaningful zero point. Thus 200° Kelvin is twice as 'warm' as 100° Kelvin, because they both relate to the same absolute-zero temperature.

Many kinds of data employed in quantitative research are ratio scales. In concept of zero velocity a series of measurements of velocity would represent **ratio data**. A velocity of 30 km/hour is three times the velocity of 10 km/hour. Marketing and sales figures also represent ratio data. In the concept of zero sales a series of figures representing sales over a period of time would constitute ratio data.

Sales figures of 10,000 would be 100 times greater than sales of only 100 items.

Thinking carefully about the type of data which we are using thus helps us to be more precise about the statistical techniques which we are entitled to employ.

One final truism about using statistics is that the results that you get are only as good as the data which you put in, and the type of analysis used. As a range of techniques statistics cannot work miracles on poorly collected data, and equally the results should not be assumed to be telling us any more than the limitations of the techniques suggest.

Descriptive statistics

One of the main functions of descriptive statistics is to take a relatively large number of measurements and then to present them in a readily understandable form. For example, survey data frequently consists of very large numbers of readings or responses, and by simply looking at a collection of numbers it is very difficult to identify trends; we need some means of summarising the data.

Suppose that you are working in educational administration, and you want to know how many full-time students are enrolled on each of the courses in a particular college. Having collected the information from all of the course leaders, you are confronted with an array of numbers, which you wish to summarise in some way. An initial strategy is to group the courses together according to the number of students enrolled, as in Figure 11.1.

This kind of tabular representation is called a **frequency distribution**, because it shows at a glance the frequency with which courses of different sizes occur. There are more courses with between 31 and 40 full-time enrolled students than any other size. The second most common size of course is that with between 21 and 30 enrolled students. There are three very small courses with only between one and ten students, and there is also one very large course, with between 81 and 90 enrolled students. If we add up the right-hand column, we obtain the total number of courses in the college, i.e. 61.

A frequency distribution such as this gives us an overview of the level of student enrolments on different courses at a glance. However, in

Number of students enrolled	Number of courses
1–10	3
11–20	8
21–30	14
31–40	22
41–50	7
51–60	2
61–70	3
71–80	1
81–90	1

Figure 11.1 Tabular representation of frequency distribution

transforming the original untreated, or raw data, into a more manageable form, we have made a number of sacrifices. For example, we do not include in the frequency distribution the names of the courses, and so in this particular presentation we do not know which subjects have the most enrolments. Secondly, from this data presentation we cannot calculate the average enrolment figure because we have not got the exact enrolment figure for any particular course. Nevertheless, there are many advantages to this type of frequency distribution. We get the kind of overall picture that it would be impossible to obtain from the raw data, and we get an idea of the way in which students are distributed from course to course across the college.

Descriptive statistics are helpful in tabular form, but are often more accessible and easier to communicate in graphical form. Perhaps the most common way in which to present a frequency distribution is in the form of a **bar chart**, in which the horizontal axis is divided according to the different categories of numbers of enrolled students, as is shown in Figure 11.2.

The vertical axis of the bar chart shown in Figure 11.2 indicates the frequency with which each of these categories occurs. It should be remembered that graphical presentations such as this are only accurate if the category intervals on the horizontal axis are of equal width or size. If they are different to each other, then a distorted picture is given. It is important to think about this when devising the original categories into which to divide the raw data.

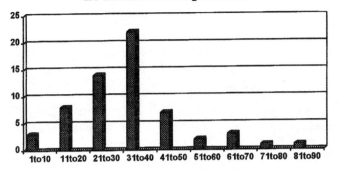

**Bar Chart showing the frequency with which students
are enrolled on college courses**

Figure 11.2 Bar-chart representation of frequency distribution

Another general strategy for describing and summarising a set of data is to calculate a number which is representative of the data. The most common way of doing this is to compute what is normally called the 'average', although statisticians prefer to use the term 'arithmetic mean', or usually just 'mean'. The problem with using the term 'average' is that it has become such a frequent part of everyday language that it has lost some of its precision. We refer to 'the average school', or to 'the average customer', for example, without necessarily having a very precise sense of what exactly is meant.

The mean is calculated by adding up all the separate measurements which comprise a collection of data, and then dividing the total figure by the number of measurements. The resulting figure has a number of important features:

- the mean is unambiguous. There is only one mean for a particular set of data;
- the calculation of the mean is straightforward;
- the mean is calculated by using each piece of numerical data; each measurement contributes to the mean.

The final characteristic given above is both a strength and a weakness. In principle, it ensures a general degree of representation, although one or two unusual or exceptional measurements can influence the mean quite considerably. Suppose, in a set of experimental readings, that one number is much lower or greater than the rest, perhaps because of experimental error. This number will still be included in the calculation for the mean, and will distort the answer.

Another method of describing the central point of a set of data is to use the descriptive statistic named the **median**. This is calculated by first arranging a set of data in order of increasing (or decreasing) magnitude. The median is then the size of the middle term in the series. Thus, in the following series of numbers,

2, 7, 9, 16, 23, 24 and 32

the size of the middle term is 16, and this number is therefore the median of the data. In this case, there is an equal number of terms on either side of the median. This particular series of terms consists of an odd number of terms; if, however, there is an even number of terms, the median is calculated by working out the mean of the two central terms. Thus, in the series of terms

1, 7, 10, 12, 17, 21

the two middle terms are 10 and 12, and the mean of these is 11. This is therefore the median number.

One advantage possessed by the median is that, unlike the mean, it remains unaffected by an extreme value: such a value is simply counted as another term used to determine the middle term.

A final means of summarising a set of data is to state the '**mode**', or 'modal value', of the data. This is simply the most common number contained in the data. In the case of the median and the mean, there is only one possible numerical value for any particular set of data. However, it is possible for there to be several different modal values for the data: there may be more than one numerical value, which is equally common, represented in a set of data.

A major advantage of the mode is that it can be used with qualitative as well as quantitative data. For example, in a market-research exercise, potentially new car buyers may be asked to name the features that they most look for in a new car. There is no way in which a mean or median can be calculated, but the modal value is the feature which is most commonly named.

One important issue which has emerged in these discussions, is that in a series of quantitative data there may be one or two extreme values, or the data may be fairly closely clustered together. We might consider for a moment two school students who obtain the following marks in five subjects during end-of-term tests.

| Student A: | 20% | 15% | 65% | 60% | 90% |
| Student B: | 55% | 45% | 50% | 53% | 47% |

A quick calculation will show that the mean of the marks for both students is the same, i.e. 50 per cent. However, there is obviously a far greater variation in the marks obtained by student A than by student B. As we are concerned only with describing this data, we will not make judgements about which set of marks we find most praiseworthy, but will confine ourselves to a statistical summary of the figures. A simple measure of the variability of the marks can be computed by calculating the range of the marks. This is, in effect, the difference between the smallest and the largest figures. For student A, the range of the marks is from 15 to 90 per cent, i.e. 75 per cent; while for student B the range is from 45 to 55 per cent, i.e. 10 per cent. For marks which have the same mean, this is a considerable difference.

In any set of data it is possible to calculate the extent to which the individual measures are spread widely from the mean, or are clustered closely to it. This involves the calculation of what we call the **standard deviation**. For any set of readings or quantitative data there is a single standard deviation. This is easily calculated by using the following steps:

1 Firstly, calculate the mean of the numbers by adding all of them together and then dividing the total by the number of separate values.
2 For each value, write down its difference from the mean: i.e. subtract the mean from the value, if the latter is greater, or subtract the value from the mean, if the mean is greater.
3 Take each difference from the mean, and multiply it by itself.
4 Add up these squared differences.
5 Divide the total by the number of original values.
6 Calculate the square root of the resulting number. This will give you the standard deviation.

A review of this procedure will show that the more the original values deviate from the mean, the more this will result in a larger number for the standard deviation; the opposite is also true. The standard deviation is a very important statistic, and is widely used in other types of analysis.

This has been a brief examination of some aspects of descriptive statistics. We will now turn to an important concept, that of correlation.

——— Correlational analysis ———

The study of correlation is concerned with the examination of the relationship between two variables. Instead of the word 'relationship', we might also, rather loosely, use the words 'connection', or 'association'.

Thus we might observe that generally cars with larger engine sizes require more petrol to travel a certain distance when compared with smaller-engined cars. Measurements may also reveal that the association is not precise. We might perhaps wonder whether this is because there may be other factors in operation, such as the weight of the car, the type of tyres, or the age of the engine. Our observations, however, generally suggest that there is a correlation between the variables of engine size and petrol consumption. This would be described as a positive correlation, because as one variable increases, the other has a corresponding tendency to increase.

Another example of a positive correlation might be the relationship between the amount of money spent on marketing a product and the sales figures for the product. We might generally find that as the marketing investment increases, so do the sales figures, at least up to a certain point. We could plot some hypothetical points on a graph, as shown in Figure 11.3.

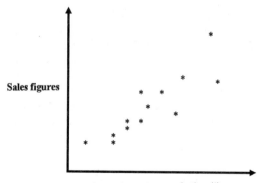

Figure 11.3   Scattergram indicating positive correlation

Each point on the graph in Figure 11.3 represents a specific amount spent on marketing and the corresponding sales figures at the time. If there was a perfectly positive correlation, then the points would all lie on a straight line. In this case they do not, because other factors clearly affect sales rather than simply the marketing budget. This type of graph is sometimes known as a **scattergram**.

An increase in one variable is not always associated with an increase in another; sometimes an increase in a variable is actually associated with a decrease in another variable. An example of such a correlation is the case of the variables 'age of a motor vehicle' and 'value of a motor vehicle'. Generally, as a motor vehicle becomes older, its value decreases. Of course, there are some exceptions to this generalisation; some people will purchase a new sports car and then keep it carefully for a number of years, knowing that if it is well preserved its value will increase. Similarly, some older versions of rare or unusual cars actually increase in value. In addition, many other variables are at work in such cases, including the condition of the bodywork, and the mileage of the engine. We can, however, say that other things being equal, the older a car, the less its value; this is termed a negative correlation. If we plotted a scattergram for these two variables, it might look something like that shown in Figure 11.4.

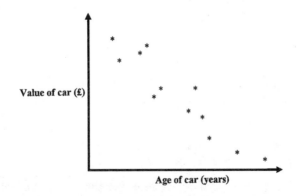

Figure 11.4 Scattergram indicating negative correlation

The points are scattered around the scattergram in Figure 11.4 because there is not a perfect negative correlation between these two variables. In an idealised case, graphs demonstrating positive and negative correlations would look like those in Figure 11.5.

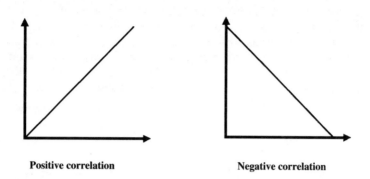

Positive correlation   Negative correlation

Figure 11.5 Graphs illustrating positive and negative correlations

Some variables may show little or no correlation, in which case a scattergram would look something like that in Figure 11.6.

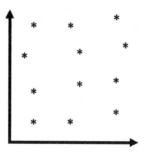

Figure 11.6 Scattergram showing no correlation

A single line representation would resemble that shown in Figure 11.7.

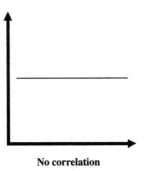

No correlation

Figure 11.7 Single-line representation showing no correlation

Two variables which are likely to be unassociated are the length of a car and the value of the car. Some short cars, such as high-performance sports cars, may be far more expensive than the longer saloon cars, or family estates. There does not appear to be a clear association between these variables.

It is possible to calculate the extent to which two variables are correlated, and this involves calculating the correlation coefficient. These vary from +1.0, in the case of a perfect positive correlation, to –1.0 in a perfect negative correlation. A coefficient of 0.0 indicates no correlation. The coefficient is a measure of the extent to which points on the graph are scattered away from an idealised straight line. A coefficient of 0.8 would indicate points fairly close to a straight line, while 0.2 would indicate fairly widely scattered points.

The final issue to mention about correlation is that just because two variables are connected, this does not mean that one variable is the cause of a change in the other. For example, if we reconsider the variables 'expenditure on marketing' and 'sales figures', we might be in a country-wide situation in which the economy is becoming healthier. This might enable a company to spend more on marketing, while sales are simultaneously increasing anyway. The two variables may seem to be causally connected, but in fact they are both influenced by another factor, i.e. the state of the economy. Caution must therefore always be exercised in assuming that correlation signifies causation.

Using computer packages

It is hard to imagine a modern researcher carrying out the sometimes tedious, and certainly complex, statistical calculations without the aid of a computer. Even hand-held scientific calculators can perform a wide range of statistical calculations. There is, of course, a school of thought that holds that understanding is better facilitated by carrying out calculations arithmetically. Certainly it is essential when using a calculator to understand fully the stages that are inherent in a calculation, even if the computer program has enabled you to omit some of the steps needed for mechanical calculation.

At their simplest level, wordprocessing packages have become sufficiently complex to enable one to input numerical data as a data tabulation, and then to display that as a histogram, pie chart or bar graph, which can often be two- or three-dimensional on the screen and print-out. These simple diagrams are very useful for summarising data.

At the other extreme of the range of sophistication are software packages such as the very widely used SPSS (Statistical Package for the Social Sciences). This enables a very wide range of elementary and advanced calculations to be carried out speedily, and with reliable accuracy. Commands, which can be used singly or in sequences, are used to instruct the software to carry out certain computations on the data. A very useful, practical guide to using SPSS is provided by Bryman and Cramer (1994; see the 'Further reading' section).

NEW CONCEPTS

Bar chart	Mode
Descriptive statistics	Nominal data
Frequency distribution	Ordinal data
Inferential statistics	Ratio data
Interval data	Scattergram
Median	Standard deviation

PRESENTING
YOUR RESULTS

12
ORAL PRESENTATIONS

─────── **An executive summary** ───────

Research is often first presented in oral form, before it is expounded at some length in a formal research report or journal article. The most typical form of oral presentation within the academic community is the conference presentation, followed by the circulation of a conference paper. The academic conference is used as a medium for academics and researchers to:

- meet with colleagues from other institutions and parts of the world who are working in the same area;
- disseminate their research findings – particularly examples of research in progress;
- stimulate the development of new ideas for research.

When academic conferences are being arranged, a '**calling notice**' for research papers is usually advertised in relevant journals, and increasingly nowadays on the Internet. Interested would-be contributors then usually send a summary of the paper that they intend to submit. These summaries are vetted by a planning group for the conference, and the selected contributors are then informed. The usual format of the conference is that each contributor delivers an oral presentation lasting between, say, 25 and 30 minutes, and then answers any questions. After that, the contributor circulates copies of a longer, typed version of their oral presentation.

Within the business and commercial sectors, employees also deliver oral presentations of data. This data might be research data which is identical to the type of material presented at an academic conference, or it might be marketing information and sales figures which, although they are primary data, are not usually presented in the guise of being research data. A written version of the material is sometimes also made available afterwards, which is often called an executive summary. The term 'executive summary' is also used when an abbreviated version of a longer research report is prepared specifically for circulation to selected people, in a form which can be easily absorbed.

The main point to note about an oral presentation is that it should not be a written report which is simply read out to the audience. The oral report is different: while it may seek to give basically the same information as the longer, formal report, it should be presented in an interesting and entertaining way. The oral report has more in common with the executive summary than the written report, in that it should be brief, and designed to allow information to be easily absorbed and, above all, that it should excite interest.

Preparing visual aids

There is nothing more likely to bore an audience than to give them a short report or executive summary, and then to proceed to read it out to them. (Indeed, this could easily be construed as a comment upon the reading abilities of the audience!)

The oral presentation should present the same information as is given in a written report but in a different way, and most importantly, in a way which motivates the audience to actually read the executive summary (and then perhaps also any longer and fuller research report).

One way in which to hold the interest of the audience is to use such visual aids as acetate slides on an overhead projector. An even more sophisticated device is to use a projector which will project the image of a computer screen directly onto a wall or screen. Whichever method is used, the essential features of the process are the same.

Suppose that the executive summary of the research project lists its aims as follows:

- to investigate the perceived relevance of a new computer-based learning package to students;
- to assess the extent to which the learning package motivates the students;
- to investigate possible amendments to the learning package.

It is not necessary to reproduce these aims in full on an acetate slide; instead they can be summarised as follows:

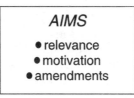

The acetate slide picks up and emphasises three key words – one taken from each of the aims. The audience can easily read these words, and can use them as a focus to help them to understand what the researcher is saying. The members of the audience can also remember such key words more easily, and can additionally relate them to the appropriate section in either the executive summary or the full research report.

Brevity and clarity

In both the oral part of the presentation and in the visual aids, the emphasis should be upon being brief and clear. When an audience is listening to an oral presentation of an academic topic, it is difficult for them to concentrate for very long, and to carry complicated ideas in their minds. It is therefore very important to distil information for a verbal presentation, and to make the arguments and knowledge content as straightforward as possible. The more sophisticated aspects of arguments can be included in the full, written report.

A similar approach should be taken with visual aids. The audience is trying both to listen to the verbal report, and also to read the visual aids. The two should thus complement each other. The skilled presenter uses a series of visual aids, both to act as a prompt for the presentation, and also to help the audience by providing an element of clarity.

It is a good idea for the presenter to arrange the visual aids in sequence, and then to use them as a prompt for the dialogue. With practice, it is often not necessary to have a script, but rather to let the dialogue develop in conjunction with the visual aids. The latter should merely show the main key words, concepts and arguments of the research. For example, there could be separate acetate slides for each of the following sections of the presentation:

- origin of the research idea
- aims
- research design and methodology
- data and data analysis
- conclusions

For some of these sections, it will probably be necessary to show a number of acetate slides, for example, for the data and data analysis section. For the others, it is more a matter of personal preference, although the emphasis should always be upon making the information as easy to absorb as possible. For example, visual aids for the research design section might be presented as shown in Figure 12.1.

Research Design 1

CASE-STUDY APPROACH

(employing an 'action-research' perspective)

Data-collection method:

- non-participant observation
- field diaries
- informal interviews
- documents
- group discussion data

Research Design 2

ETHICAL ISSUES

- subject consent
- informing subjects
- recording data
- using documents for secondary purposes

Figure 12.1 Examples of visual aids

Sometimes members of an audience ask if they can have photocopies of acetates; they often regard them as being very useful summaries of a research account, simply because they are brief and clear. These can be conveniently distributed immediately at the end of the talk. However, it is often a good idea to inform the audience that they will be available later, in order to save people the effort of making notes.

— Explaining research implications —

A good way in which to conclude your talk is by asking if anyone has any questions. Alternatively, the researcher can ask the audience for feedback, asking such questions as:

- Do you think I approached the sampling question appropriately?
- Have I taken into account all of the possible threats to validity?
- Could I have designed the research in a different way?
- Is the data subject to other interpretations?
- Are there any research studies which could lead on from this?

The advantage of asking specific questions such as these, is that the audience becomes involved. Instead of just passively listening to an account of the research, they are thus encouraged to think actively about the implications. The discussion which will invariably ensue will be useful for the audience, and also for the researcher. Many interesting ideas may emerge, and it can be a good idea to have large sheets of paper ready on a flip chart, in order to record the main ideas that arise. Summarising these ideas encourages the audience, and also provides a permanent record for the researcher.

———— Suggestions for policy ————

One of the most important aspects of practical research is that it should improve the world in some way. A lot of research sets out explicitly to do this: action research, for example, has the specific intention of taking a practical issue or problem, and then investigating it in order to develop proposals for change.

Although it is sometimes argued that 'pure' research is impractical, and is merely concerned with the advancement of knowledge for its own sake, this is not necessarily true. We might take as an example research into ancient history. It may seem as though archaeological research into ancient cultures has very little to contribute to everyday problems, yet our lives are constructed upon our history. An understanding of our predecessors can help us to understand ourselves. Although some aspects of our lives are very different now, particularly in terms of technological progress, many of the issues of human existence remain much the same: life, death, distribution of resources, wealth, power, status, and many other features of human existence go on and on.

One argument is therefore that research of any kind has some implications for the betterment of life. It is no bad thing for a researcher to pause and think, at the end of a research project, for ways in which the research results might help society or individuals. In the case of research involving a commercial product, for instance, there are often many ways in which research might have an impact on policy:

- marketing and sales data might have implications for sales policy;
- feedback from customers and clients can have clear implications for production or product design;
- research data on quality and fitness for purpose can have implications for product research and development.

We increasingly need well-designed research in order to help us to understand the present, and to plan for the future.

NEW CONCEPT

Calling notice

13
WRITTEN RESEARCH REPORTS

The purpose of reports

Most people who have carried out a research investigation want to convey its results to others: there is an almost natural inclination to want other people, or colleagues, to read about what has probably taken you a considerable amount of time and effort. If you have undertaken some research in the workplace, then you will almost certainly wish to gain credit from that by showing it to your immediate superiors or line managers.

Quite apart from the natural tendency to wish to show our work to others, there is perhaps a more fundamental reason why it is important to circulate the results of research to colleagues. The entire research process is concerned with trying to add something (however small and insignificant) to the sum total of human knowledge. In order to make this worthwhile and valid, academic colleagues must have an opportunity to evaluate what we have written about. Without the general approval of the academic community, what we have worked on may not receive the wide circulation that we might wish for.

The main way in which researchers seek to disseminate their findings is through the medium of the formal research report. The usual format for this is that employed in the wide range of academic journals which cover all of the main subject areas of research. Such journals are often entitled 'The Journal of Research in . . . ' or something similar. They are typically published two or three times a year, and each issue includes perhaps half-a-dozen research reports or articles, and several pages of reviews of books that are relevant to the subject area.

Each individual journal has its own requirements for the submission of articles, but throughout the academic world there is a fairly standard format, which is described later. Differences between the various journals are usually relatively minor features, such as the style of referencing, or the length requirements for submissions. These requirements are usually printed very clearly in the journal, under such a heading as 'Notes for contributors'.

Most journals tend to follow the same procedure with regard to submissions. The approximate sequence of events resulting in publication is as follows.

1 The article is submitted to the journal's editor in the prescribed format. Most articles are 'unsolicited', although editors often do not mind being consulted in general terms about a proposed article. For instance, they are normally willing to provide advice on whether a proposed topic for an article is appropriate for that particular journal.

2 When the article is received by the editor, it is read with a view to appreciating the nature of the research, and is then sent to (usually) two independent **reviewers**, who are qualified and experienced in the subject area. The name of the author is deleted prior to sending the article for review, in order to preserve the author's anonymity, and also to ensure the impartiality of the reviewers. The latter could be placed in a rather difficult situation if they received an article from an academic or researcher who was personally known to them.

3 The reviewers then complete an assessment of the research submission, based upon criteria previously determined by the journal's editorial or management board. The article is returned to the editor, along with one of a number of possible recommendations, that:

- the article be accepted;
- the article be accepted subject to minor amendments;
- the article be extensively revised and then accepted subject to reassessment by either the editor or reviewers;
- the article be rejected.

4 The editor reads the reviewers' assessments and recommendations,

and takes the appropriate action. The decision is conveyed in writing to the author, without revealing the names of the reviewers.

5　The final stage is, of course, publication. Most journals plan their issues for some considerable time into the future, in order to make sure there are sufficient articles per issue. This means that an author may have some time to wait before seeing the article in print. It would not be unusual to have to wait for 12 months after the original submission before the article is published.

This process may be lengthy, but when an article is accepted for publication the author has the reassurance of knowing that it has been subjected to a rigorous process. Prior to its publication it will have been read and approved by probably three people (the editor and two reviewers), and will have been carefully proofread for any minor errors in spelling and syntax. This also means that when you read an article reporting research in a journal you know it has been through a fairly exacting process of quality control. This is, of course, no absolute guarantee of the validity of the research, but at the very least you know something of the procedure to which the article has previously been subjected.

Not all researchers will have the time or inclination to write up their research in this way, of course, or to seek to get it published. For many people, it may be sufficient to produce a brief summary of their research, and to circulate it among their colleagues for comment. There is also a variety of less formal publications, such as professional magazines and journals, which publish brief summaries of ongoing research. These summaries are perhaps less demanding to write, and can be produced more rapidly.

Whatever written outlet you choose for your research, a very important principle applies: the idea that research is not, at the end of the day, a private activity, but should be reported to professional colleagues. Only in this way can there be full and proper discussion about the research and its implications. Other people working in your subject area or profession thus have a chance to read and analyse your work and then, if they wish, to try to replicate the results. This is, in a sense, the final vindication of any research study. If a fellow professional can repeat your study under as similar circumstances as possible, and can obtain the same, or very similar, results, then this goes a very long way indeed to affirming your findings.

Such replication of research also provides an opportunity for others to suggest ways in which the research can either be improved, or extended by developing new investigations. In fact, in many academic journals, you will sometimes read a running debate between two academics, in which someone comments in one issue on research reported in the previous issue, and later the original researcher responds to that critique. Sometimes such a debate extends over several issues, and makes very interesting reading – it is all part of the great academic debate!

—— Structure of a research report ——

In theory, there is nothing to stop you from writing about your research in any way that you choose. Your report can be of any length and in any format that you wish. However, there is always a draw-back in doing things in a very individualistic and idiosyncratic way, particularly in the academic world. Firstly, you may find that others do not treat your research very seriously because it does not adhere to the accepted academic conventions. Secondly, you may run the danger of omitting significant aspects of the research, simply because you do not have a structure within which to work. If you are relatively new to research, it is certainly better to adopt a standard approach, and then perhaps to vary it a little as you read more widely and get new ideas for research reports. With a fairly standard format you will, at least, not go too far wrong. The following subheadings and sequence are reasonably standard, although you will probably find many variations of them.

A standard format for a research report

1 Title page

The title page should state the title of the research project, the name of the author, and any other relevant information, such as the name of a sponsoring body. For example:

An investigation of new marketing strategies for holidays
in Florida

by

John S. Vacation

with support from

The University of the Southern States

and

West Atlantic Holidays Ltd

2 Abstract

The **abstract** is a brief summary, or precis, of the entire research report. It should summarise the context of the research, its aims, methodology, results and conclusion. It is intended to give the readers of the report a concise grasp of what has been done, and what may be expected by reading the full report. An average abstract will probably be 200–300 words in length, and certainly not more than one side of A4 paper when wordprocessed with double spacing. If you examine an article in a journal, you will probably find the abstract printed in italics at the beginning of the article, perhaps occupying one-third of a page in fairly small typeface and narrowly spaced format.

3 Rationale and context

You could alternatively entitle this section simply 'Introduction'. In this section, you should explain the entire background to the research idea, and how it first came about. There is so much that you could put into this section, but here are a few suggestions:

- explain how the idea first arose in your mind and give the original stimulus for the research;
- describe what you think will be gained from the research. Explain the benefits which will accrue from it. These might include extending our understanding; helping us to provide a better service to clients or fellow professionals; or making better-informed policy decisions;
- explain where the research was conducted and the nature of the sample. This can simply be an overview;
- finally, list the aims of the research. These may be presented in a variety of ways, but my own preference is for precise statements which state very clearly what will be achieved. If you are unsure of how to express the aims, simply write down what you expect to know after the research has been carried out which you did not know before.

Examples of the way in which aims may be phrased are as follows:

- to investigate the effects on sales figures of an innovative marketing strategy;
- to compare the distribution of sales in different parts of the country;
- to contrast the sales figures of two new products.

4 Literature review

This section should review the previous work done in the field, and should:

- set your investigation in its context;
- explain how it builds upon previous research;
- give examples of existing literature and publications in related fields;
- give a sense of continuity to your research.

5 Methodology

This section should explain:

- the conceptual framework for the research, including the actual concepts used;

- the research design, its choice and justification for this particular approach;
- the data-collection method, the reasons for its choice, ethical issues, the way in which it was carried out, any difficulties involved, and the ways used to overcome them;
- the sampling strategy, and a discussion of the rationale for the choice of sample;
- the types of data collected;
- the ways used to analyse the data;
- the computer packages used;
- the ways used to present the data.

6 Results

You should present the main research findings in this section, using a style which is easy to understand. When presenting your results, the following points should be considered:

- there is no need to present all of the primary data; this should be summarised wherever possible;
- try to use diagrams, tables, histograms, graphs or pie charts to make the data as digestible as possible for the reader;
- try to be as clear as possible about what can and what cannot be inferred from the data.

7 Conclusion and recommendations

The conclusion should relate the findings to the original aims of the research, and should indicate the extent to which the aims have been achieved. It is also a good idea to indicate any possible areas for future investigation. The recommendations should focus upon any practical aspects of policy development which might be affected by the research findings.

8 References

The references, also often titled 'Further reading' should include all the works such as books and research reports, mentioned in the text. It is important to use a standard referencing system, such as the **Harvard system**, and to list books in the alphabetical order of the authors' surnames.

9 Appendices

It is best not to make the appendices too long or voluminous. The appendix should not be a repository for any document which has only tenuous connections with the research. The appendix might include copies of short documents; examples of data-collection instruments, or specific material regarding the context of the research.

—— Keeping to the essentials ——

After reading the previous section, it may seem that there is an enormous amount to put into a research report. In a sense this is so; you could potentially write a great deal. However, it is important to remember that it is a report, and not an essay or a dissertation. The readers of your report are not likely to want to read a long, discursive account; they will probably want to understand the essentials of your research as quickly as possible. On the other hand, it is important to include sufficient detail for readers to be able to repeat a version of the research if they wish to. A compromise in terms of length and detail is therefore necessary. Some general ways of achieving a succinct approach are to:

1 enumerate the points wherever possible, using numbers, or symbols such as bullet points; this is particularly true of the aims. It is easier to absorb information in this form. This approach can also be used for recommendations;
2 in the literature review, keep to those key points of the work which are relevant to your study alone. Do not try to provide a precis of the entire book;
3 in the methodology section, it is not necessary to discuss all the possible methodologies and research designs, gradually eliminating each one, and then explaining the details of that selected. Simply explain the selected approach, and say why it was chosen;
4 in the data-analysis section, there is no need to present pages and pages of primary data. This is very tedious for the reader, who will probably need to expend a lot of time in understanding what has been done by the researcher. It is much better to summarise the data, but at the same time to provide an explanation of how the data was collected;

5 in the references section, it is sometimes a good idea to divide references into groups, according to the subject matter. For example, you might try to group together works on methodology under a separate subheading, and also to do the same for works on the specific subject matter of your research. It is then easier for the reader to locate the references.

Writing style

The convention with research reports is to write in a fairly formal, impersonal way. The main purpose of this approach is to maintain an objective stance which as far as possible removes or eliminates subjective, personal comments by the researcher or author. Thus, there is a tendency to use such phrases as:

The investigation was conducted . . .

rather than

I carried out the research . . .

and

A survey was the preferred methodological approach . . .

rather than

I decided to adopt the survey approach . . .

The basic rule is to use the third-person singular rather than the first-person singular. This style of writing was probably much influenced by the empirical, positivistic approach to research, which took as its exemplar the laboratory approach to science, which makes it possible to eliminate experimenter influences and effects to some extent. This is much more difficult in the social sciences, however, in which research is very much a human, interpersonal activity, and data is usually collected from human subjects rather than from test tubes or conical flasks. Human subjects are very sensitive to the way in which they are treated during the research process, and the researcher has to make decisions about conducting the research, communicating with subjects and, in particular, about ethical procedures when collecting data.

This means that it is rather erroneous to pretend that human-focused research is highly objective and impersonal. In many ways it is, in fact, very subjective. There is thus an argument for softening the writing style of the report somewhat, and to thus reflect something of this subjectivity.

It is really a matter of achieving a sensible balance. A research report is not a novel or a short story, and we must retain a good deal of the 'scientific' element in the writing. However, there are places in which the first-person approach may be appropriate, such as:

- in the introduction, in which you are describing the context in which you are working and collecting research data, e.g. describing your school or company;
- in the literature review, in which you may wish to reflect certain preferences for particular approaches to research;
- when indicating the choice of methodology, when you may wish to relate the choice process to what you know about the sample of people who provided the data. In other words, you can explain how you came about selecting the methodology which you considered suitable for your subjects;
- in the section on recommendations, in which you may wish to show how the suggestions that you make reflect your own, personal interpretation of the significance of the results;
- finally, in what is sometimes called a 'reflexive account'. Many authors are now including a personal academic and research autobiography in their research reports. The purpose of this is to show how the personal background of the researcher impacts upon the collection and interpretation of the data.

Some people may fear that a trend towards a rather more personal element in reporting research may result in a loss of academic rigour. This is obviously a serious concern. On the other hand, the inclusion of more personal comments can be interpreted as being a very open and honest form of research reporting, which lays bare, as far as possible, the nature of the research process. According to this view, this trend represents an enhancement of academic rigour.

There will never be a precise answer to the question of writing style, nor will there be styles of research reporting with which everyone will be in agreement. There are also particular styles of methodology which tend to attract certain approaches to research reporting. Experimental and survey researchers tend to write, on the whole, in a formal, traditional style. On the other hand, research conducted in, say, the action-research mode is sometimes reported in a more personal, subjective style.

One way of finding a style which is both academically acceptable and also suits you is to read a number of articles and research reports within the style of research which you are using. As long as they have been published in an academic journal, then you know that they have been through the reviewing process outlined earlier, and that they represent the accepted form of presentation of at least one 'school' of researchers. You are thus safe in following that particular format.

Whichever process and writing style you decide to adopt, you will find that all research reports in one way or another adhere to the structure outlined earlier, and have a writing style which describes the research clearly and in such a way that someone else could replicate it. This is really the basis of a sound research report.

Circulation

When starting to write a research report, it is worth thinking about the possible circulation of the report, because that can affect the writing style. When the report is completed, it can be very useful to produce a brief report in a professional format on a computer, and then to circulate it to professional colleagues. This can have some advantages, as follows:

- your research will be read;
- you may receive comments and feedback on what you have written;
- you may receive offers of collaboration on a future investigation in a similar area;
- you may receive correspondence and communication from interested researchers whom you did not realise were working in the same area, helping to create research networks;
- you can let people know of the areas in which you are working;
- you may receive invitations to write up the research in a more formal way for a journal or an edited book.

These advantages also apply to publishing your research, with the added benefit that publishing attracts a degree of immediate status. A published report has greater credibility, because your colleagues know that it has been through a process of peer review. In addition, publishing attracts a wider circulation and readership.

When you are disseminating your research, however, there are a number of important questions to consider. These tend to revolve around questions of permission and confidentiality.

Permission to publish

Whether you are circulating a research report privately, or are seeking to publish it, there are important considerations to think about, involving permission to publicise research. In all research involving the collection of data from people it is important to consider the following issues:

- you should adhere to any agreement that was reached with the subjects when they provided data. If you promised that you would report the research in a certain way, then you should adhere to that promise;
- subjects should have been informed of any intention to publicise the data;
- if the data was collected in an institution, was there an agreement about how the research would be reported? It is probably better to have such an agreement, even if you think that it would not be possible to identify the institution. Complete anonymity is often very difficult to achieve;
- where an institution is concerned, there may also be a danger of inadvertently conveying material of commercial sensitivity. Even if the precise identity of the institution is not disclosed, it may still be possible for competitor organisations to glean information from a research report. Institutions therefore usually appreciate sensitivity when material that is related to their organisation is published, and it is usually better from both the researcher's and institution's viewpoint to have a clear agreement on the matter.

Issues of confidentiality

When writing a research report, it is usually preferable to ensure the anonymity of both the individuals and organisations mentioned in the report. This secures the peace of mind of both the researcher and the subject of the research.

Sometimes a subject will say that they do not mind their name being used. This may apply to both an individual or an organisation. However, the subject will probably not have read the report when this is said, and may not have thought out all the possible implications. It is possible that they may later regret giving their permission, and may argue that they had no idea of the content of the report. They may argue that if they had known the content of the report they would never have given their permission.

In some countries, it is the norm to be quite sensitive to these matters, and also to consider litigation more frequently if one is unhappy about the content of such a report. This can place the researcher in a very difficult situation, and they may feel the necessity to show the report to everyone who is named therein, and to ask for their approval. This is really very difficult for the researcher, because it is frequently impossible to get the approval of everyone. In any case, it is encroaching upon the academic independence of the researcher who, at the end of the day, must attach their own name to the report. When this is done, the responsibility for the content rests firmly with the researcher.

It may therefore seem a fairly simple matter to mention the names of individuals and organisations if they give their approval, but the situations resulting from this can become very complex. For these reasons, it is probably better to use some device with which to try to mask the identity of the respondents. It is sometimes argued that the use of such strategems devalues the research in some way, because the reader of the report does not know to whom it applies. There is an element of truth in this argument, but any inherent difficulties can be circumvented by providing details of either the individual or the organisation which has provided the data. If all of the relevant contextual information is provided, then it is possible for the reader of the report to understand the relevance of the research to other settings. In the case of individuals providing data, some of the relevant contextual information may include their:

- age;
- gender;
- ethnic group;
- type of employment;
- type and location of residence.

Relevant contextual details for organisations may include the:

- physical description of their buildings;
- location;
- access;
- products manufactured;
- number of employees;
- management structure.

When describing features such as location, it is obviously important not to name the real location in terms of state, county or street name. Coupled with other details, this could easily enable an organisation to be identified. A description such as 'a rural area of southern England', or 'a large industrial city in the eastern United States' may well suffice.

This kind of contextual information enables the reader of the report to generalise the data to other, relatively similar contexts, and to relate to situations with which they are familiar.

If it is decided to maintain confidentiality and **anonymity**, there are a number of strategies and devices that can be used in the report, such as the following.

1 If the research involves any type of case study, then it is possible to refer to the subject as the Respondent (with a capital 'R'), or as the Organisation (with a capital 'O').

2 Respondent A and Respondent B, or Organisation 1 and Organisation 2. This is a neutral type of terminology, but suffers from a lack of realism, and can make the report sound rather official or formal.

3 In many ways, the best technique is to use fictional names. The main advantage in this is that it gives the report an air of reality. The reader can make an association with the name, and it tends to bring the subject(s) of the research to life in the minds of readers. There are, however, one or two potential snags. It is important that the invented name is realistic, but that it should not include any value association. For example, in devising a name for a company which manufactures denim clothing, one should avoid a name like 'Cut-price Jeans' unless the real name of the company suggests a budget approach to marketing and selling. Also, in the case of individuals, the name should reflect as closely as possible the main features of the real name in terms of:

- gender implications;
- ethnic group implications;
- frequency of use of the name.

In other words, any fictional names used should reflect the study population as accurately as possible.

A written research report is the means by which you present your work to the world. It is therefore worth taking a lot of care over its design and writing.

NEW CONCEPTS

Abstract	Harvard system
Anonymity	Reviewer

14

FURTHER RESEARCH

Limitations of a research investigation

We use the word 'research' in a great variety of ways in everyday language. For example, we hear many people treating the idea of research as if it were a self-validating process: people will sometimes use such expressions as:

Research shows us that . . .

or even

Research proves that . . .

The implication behind such use of language is that research is such a rigorous process, conducted by people who are not envisaged as being capable of error, that it yields truths about the world which cannot, and should not, be challenged.

This perception of research tends to be highly respectful towards a public image of academics and scientists, who are generally considered to operate on a different level to that of the non-academic. The problem with this image of research is that it does not challenge in any way the nature of either the research or the researcher. It simply assumes that both are separate from the 'ordinary' way of looking at the world.

Of course, there is one way of thinking about research which is not too far removed from this perception. The scientist in the laboratory may well be adding to an understanding of a very narrow and complex area of science, and it may be true that only a small group of other specialists would be able to appreciate the work being done. However, such specialist work is only likely to add a very small element to our total understanding of the mechanisms of the universe. Even specialist academic research is normally only incremental, adding one tiny facet of knowledge to our understanding. Only extremely rarely does anyone, such as a Newton or Einstein conduct research which results in a completely fresh vision of the universe.

The vast majority of research is extremely limited in its scale and scope, and is generally insufficient in terms of its data to be able to state results categorically. Usually it requires much more work in order to corroborate or refute the earlier findings.

The word 'research' is also used, however, in other, less specific and less formally academic ways in our language. We can say, for example:

He is carrying out research for a new novel.

This implies that an author is doing some background reading, and is perhaps checking up on a few facts. The author may also be interviewing people, and may possibly be visiting locations which will be used in the novel, in order to be able to describe them faithfully. This is obviously a very different interpretation of 'research' when compared to that of the scientist in the laboratory. There is no implication of esoteric, specialist knowledge, but rather the implication that any reasonably intelligent person could conduct this 'research'. Nevertheless, there is also the assumption that the research is being conducted in a systematic way, and that a careful attempt is being made to amass accurate information, and to check for authenticity wherever possible.

Finally, there is a very everyday sense in which the word research can be used, such as:

She is researching ways of piping away that water in the garden.

This implies that there is here a problem to be solved, and that it is being investigated in order to find a solution. There is no implication that this type of research requires any special knowledge or understanding, merely an intelligent, systematic approach to problem-solving. There are, of course, many everyday situations in which this type of use of the word 'research' would not seem out of place.

The word 'research' can thus be legitimately applied to very many contexts, and can be used to refer to both a specialised pursuit of knowledge and to a much more general, problem-solving situation. All such uses of the word are, however, characterised by a step-by-step, logical approach, and a clear idea of the problem or issue requiring solution. Moreover, there is also a sense in which research as an activity never actually locates a solution. Research implies a sense of travelling hopefully, and of perhaps getting very close to a solution, but stopping short of absolute certainty.

The principal reason for this implication is the continued possibility of new data being collected. No matter how sure we are that the sun will rise tomorrow, it remains a logical possibility that one day it will fail to rise. This kind of logical possibility in research is inherent in all empirically based findings, and the tiny degree of uncertainty provides the provisional nature of all empirical-research conclusions.

———— Applying the results ————

Research is of enormous value to society, but not just in the sense of the specialist making a very specific contribution to knowledge. This is not to say, however, that this is not important: indeed, in the popular imagination it is probably the main function of research. The discovery of a new chemical process; the synthesis of a new drug; the development of a new medical technique; the manufacture of a new type of semi-conductor; these are all the types of activity which most people probably think of when research comes to mind. Such activities generally involve an advance in knowledge, and moreover an advance which has a practical application.

Nevertheless, research has many functions in society other than the specialist accumulation of knowledge. One function is in enabling government to develop policy. Governments require an enormous amount of systematic information about the population if they are to develop sound policy. Research in this area may include such activities as:

● researching the way in which families spend their disposable income;
● researching people's leisure activities;
● documenting the patterns of continuing education and training in the population;

- researching the geographical mobility of the population in relation to employment opportunities;
- researching the connection between educational qualifications and employment.

When applying research, there is sometimes a tendency to assume that the researcher has insights that are perhaps lacking in others. If we take this particular view too far, then we can allow research and researchers to assume a level of power and authority which they perhaps should not wield.

It has been a theme of this book that research results are provisional at best, and should not be accorded absolute authority. It is mistaken to use research results as a justification for policy decisions, by using phrases such as, 'research in this field makes it perfectly clear that . . .'. We should be rightly suspicious when we read such pronouncements: such expressions seek to arrogate an authority which they simply do not possess.

The authority of research, and of research findings, resides not in the researcher, or in the organisation supporting the research, but in the systematic, objective way in which the research is conducted, and also in the dispassionate, balanced way in which it is reported. This is the true strength of the research process. Research presented like this does not seek to create arguments from authority, but merely to present its findings for public scrutiny.

— Developing organisational policy —

Research has an enormous contribution to make to the development of organisational policy. There is an increasing tendency for organisations to try to clarify their goals and objectives. This approach often manifests itself in the publication of a mission statement which, besides setting broad organisational targets, also outlines the general values and parameters within which the organisation functions.

Such mission statements tend to be very general, and perhaps sometimes a little Utopian, but they do provide an indication for shareholders, employees, managers and clients, of the general direction in which the company envisages itself moving.

The major step for an organisation is to move from a mission statement to specific strategies designed to meet those goals, and there are a variety of ways in which such strategies can be identified. A particular line of action may have been used in another company, for example, and it may be decided to try it. It is possible in this way for a particular strategy to spread from organisation to organisation, on the assumption that if it is being used elsewhere then it must be useful. Other sources of ideas include practices which have been adopted in other countries; strategies recommended by government departments; or ideas found in recently published books. The general fallacy with all of these approaches, however, is that just because an idea works in one context, in conjunction with a particular set of economic and social factors, does not mean that it will necessarily work elsewhere.

An entirely different approach to developing strategies is to base these upon research findings. Let us consider the case of a company which is developing a new training policy for its employees, including the need to provide a range of formal qualifications. Instead of copying the policy of other, competitor companies, the organisation could use a research-based strategy initially to try to determine the staff-training needs of the organisation. The starting point would be to use a research-based approach to determine the skills required in order to produce the company's products. In many organisations, this issue is often dealt with on an *ad hoc* basis, e.g. there is a feeling that another computing expert is needed. A research approach would, however, start with a survey of all of the skills needed in the organisation. The second stage is then to conduct a staff audit to identify which of these skills are currently possessed by the staff. Any deficiency in skills is thus clearly identified as a shortfall between those skills needed and those possessed by the staff.

The third stage is to examine the shortfall, and ask a number of questions, as follows.

- Is the skill shortage among only a few staff, or is it widely spread?
- Is the shortage best remedied with in-house training by existing staff, or are outside experts needed?
- Would it be appropriate to seek qualifications or certification for staff, or is this unnecessary?
- What would be the costs of remedying this shortfall?
- How could we assess the productivity and efficiency gains of providing such training programmes?

Each of these questions is, in effect, another research issue. For example, in order to answer the second question, it may be necessary to interview some existing employees in order to ascertain whether they would be able to organise the necessary training courses. The interviews would need to establish aspects of the qualifications held, and also the potential level of teaching and training skills possessed by employees. There would also be the need to collect data on the issue's management aspects. There will be replacement costs involved in taking people away from their regular duties and asking them to plan training courses. Research will also have to be undertaken into the costs of engaging external 'experts' in the field.

Even though this is a fairly complex question, it is nevertheless possible to use a research-based approach to separate the issues, and to collect data on them individually. This approach may not yield an answer which is absolutely certain, but it is systematic and logical. Its strength lies in the notion that when the final decision is made it will be known upon what data it was based.

Once it has been decided exactly how to structure the training programme, it will be necessary for the organisation to monitor the changes in efficiency and profitability that result, and to relate these to the money invested in training.

Research feedback cycles

It is never easy to know whether an innovation in an organisation is good value for money in terms of improving effectiveness or efficiency. A research approach could be used to evaluate a training programme in a variety of ways, as follows:

- employees could be interviewed after the course to try to find out whether they feel that their skills have improved, or whether their knowledge has been enhanced;
- productivity levels could be monitored and related to the training programme. This will not be easy, and the arguments previously discussed about causal connections are relevant here. It will be difficult to make certain connections between training and productivity, but it should be possible to build up a general picture;
- job performance could be observed and monitored after the training;

- a survey of managers could be conducted, in order to collect data on their opinions.

All of this data should enable trainers and managers to build up a picture of the value of the training courses. Such feedback from research is helpful in terms of the specific issue being investigated, but it also provides a range of information which may be useful to the organisation. Among other things, it encourages a culture of self-reflection and self-evaluation, which can be very positive for organisations.

—— A research-based culture ——

An organisational culture which is founded upon a research approach has certain characteristics which affect both the organisation and the individuals who work within it. First of all, it tends towards the rational, in terms of decision- and policy-making: the reasons for actions are clearly thought out and documented, and are based upon a clear analysis of the relevant data. This is not to say that the reasons employed as justification are necessarily the best, or the only reasons, but at least the organisation has made the origin of those reasons clear.

In a research-based culture, there is a much more restricted application of examples of ideological reasons or decision-making, or of people seeking to provide arguments based upon their personal feelings or preferences. If individuals do subscribe to a particular ideology, the culture demands that they bring this out into the open and acknowledge how it affects their decision-making. It is probably too much to expect that an organisation can be totally free of ideology, but a research-based culture minimises this by expecting an open and honest appraisal of issues.

Such a culture is as objective as possible. The purpose of meetings and discussions is not seen as an opportunity for confrontation between different parties, but rather to explore possible options in a balanced way. In this sense, discussion is depersonalised. A meeting is seen as an exchange of ideas, rather than as a competition between the ideas held by particular people; the ideas are separated from the people who support them. There is the expectation that individuals will not single-mindedly support only their preferred option, but will carefully evaluate all of the possible options before making a final choice. Such evaluations are also based upon research evidence. The methodology is made clear, and the process of analysis is subjected to public and peer scrutiny.

This type of culture has an important effect upon the way in which individuals conduct themselves within the organisation, and upon the nature of interpeer discourse. There tends to be much less of a sense of competition between individuals, because individuals are seen less as the sponsors of a particular idea than as evaluators of all ideas. In this type of culture decision-making is not private but public. The criteria for making a decision are public, and in addition the data collected and methods of analysis used are in the public domain. Discourse with a research-based culture becomes much less a case of strongly advocating a favoured strategy, but rather of engaging in an open and objective analysis of ideas.

This is a vision of what research can do for an organisation. Its value resides not so much in the acquisition of new knowledge and skills, but in the research process itself. In discussing the purposes of co-operative inquiry and research, Reason (1988, p.222; see the 'Further reading' section) writes:

> It shows that human inquiry is not simply a way of generating academic knowledge, but is an approach to personal and professional practice – a way of learning through risk-taking in living. It again emphasises the holistic purpose of human inquiry to develop understanding for worthwhile action in human situations.

Research is not so much a product but a process. Therein lies its value. The significance of research as a process is that it encourages us to be different people. It encourages us to be objective rather than subjective; fair and balanced instead of competitive; value-neutral instead of ideological; and dispassionate instead of self-interested. These are worthwhile goals, although not easy to achieve. However, research as a process encourages us in this direction.

—— Developing new investigations ——

When we see research as a process rather than a product, then it is clearly endless. We never reach that point when there is nothing more worth investigating or inquiring into. Research and systematic enquiry become a way of life, rather than, say, a part of one's job.

Research is also an extremely practical activity. In the popular imagination, research is often linked to theory as something which is set apart from everyday life. Nothing could be further from the truth. Research usually starts from the existence of a practical problem about which certain questions must be asked.

How can we achieve a certain goal, given our limited resources?
Is it fair to act in such a way?
What is the most efficient way of making something?
Why do people in those circumstances behave in that particular way?

Questions can always be answered in one form or another, to some degree of accuracy. However, if we aspire to answers which have weighed up all of the issues, and have tried to take the balanced view, then we need the approach of research. We can always come up with explanations, hypotheses and theories, and we can do so very quickly if we are not too worried about the level of sophistication used, or the resulting validity. But if we want the most accurate and truthful picture of the world to which we may aspire, then we must follow the path of research, and must never stop seeking out the best ways in which to explain and understand our surroundings.

GLOSSARY

Abstract a summary of a research report. In academic journals, the abstract is printed at the beginning of the article, and is usually 100 to 150 words in length

Access in a field-research context, the word is used in terms of being able to make contact with possible respondents. It is sometimes difficult to gain access because of the influence of so-called 'gate-keepers'

Action research an approach to research which tends to focus upon the resolution or improvement of practical situations. Issues at work often provide the subject for action-research projects. The purpose is to use the research process as a practical means of intervention

Aims in a research context, aims are the goals of the research. The aims represent the knowledge and understanding which the researcher hopes to have acquired by the end of the research

Analysis of data the process by which the researcher seeks to summarise, review and understand the data which has been collected. Analysis may involve the categorising of data, and also the search for patterns and regularity. In addition, the data may be reviewed in terms of how well it supports the hypothesis or hypotheses proposed at the beginning of the project. Analysis increasingly involves the use of computer software

Anonymity ensuring that the names of respondents in a research study are not disclosed. The usual strategy is to use fictional names for respondents. It is also often the practice to employ fictional names for organisations and commercial companies

Autobiography an account or diary of a period in someone's life, can be used as research data in two ways. His or her own diary firstly may be used by the author-researcher as data for a personal, reflective account; alternatively, a researcher may use the autobiographies of others as research data

Bar chart a simple, graphical means of showing fluctuations in a variable

Calling notice the organisers of a research conference will invite speakers some time in advance by circulating publicity asking for papers

Case study an approach to research which takes as its subject a single example, or 'case'. A case study may focus on a single individual; on a group of individuals who are connected in some way; on an organisation or department within it; or say, on a geographical area. The case to be studied is selected by the researcher because it has some particular significance or interest

Category a section or group into which data is placed during analysis. Data within a single category is usually linked by a particular concept or theoretical idea

Causal connection a link between two variables whereby a change in one variable is hypothesised to be caused by a change in the other

Conceptual analysis a process of analysing spoken and written language, with a particular focus upon the ways in which people employ words and ideas

Correlation the relationship between two variables

Dependent variable this is a variable whose fluctuations are hypothesised to be caused by changes in another variable (the independent variable)

Descriptive statistics basic statistical methods which concentrate on summarising trends and changes in variables, rather than on exploring connections between variables

Elite interview an interview sampling approach in which those interviewees selected are individuals who are assumed to have special insights into, and knowledge of, the topic concerned

Empirical refers to any kind of data collected by observation or experiment, in contrast to data or research involving the conceptual analysis of language

Ethics in research terms, a concern with such issues as the feelings and privacy of respondents, and with the possible consequences for people of reporting research

Ethnographic research A research approach which attempts to provide a detailed description and analysis of a social setting, the people who are part of that setting, and the way in which they interact.

The approach has to some extent developed from anthropological studies. Ethnography places considerable emphasis upon the views of the research respondents

Executive summary   a precis of a research report for wider distribution

Field research   the process of a researcher visiting a social setting in order to collect data. The 'field' may be a school classroom, a business organisation, or any location from which data is to be collected

Frequency distribution   a summary of fluctuations in a variable within a sample

Gate-keeper   a person whose permission must be sought by the researcher in order to gain access to respondents

Generalisation   a statement which seeks to summarise research observations or changes in a variable. This may be an early stage in the process of developing a theory

Grounded theory   an approach to social-science research which seeks to use data to generate practical, usable theories, that are relevant to a particular context

Harvard system   a system of referencing widely used in academic publishing

Hypothesis   a proposed relationship between variables. Hypotheses are usually generated at an early stage in a research design, and data is subsequently collected in order to 'test' them. If the hypothesis appears to be correct, it is more accurate to say that it has been 'provisionally supported' rather than 'proven'

Ideology   a belief system or world view which is held to be 'true' by adherents. The nature of an ideology makes it difficult either to support or negate by means of scientific enquiry

Independent variable   this is the variable which is hypothesised as the cause of changes in the dependent variable

Inferential statistics   the branch of statistics concerned with evaluating the relationships between variables, and also the extent to which a sample is characteristic of a population as a whole

Informed consent   a principle of ethics in research which argues that all potential respondents should have full details about the research project and possible consequences before giving their agreement to take part in it

Interpretive approach   research in which considerable emphasis is placed by the researcher upon the views and perceptions of the respondents taking part in the research

Interval data   data which can be arranged in order of magnitude, and where the numerical difference between values is known. The measurement scale used has equal intervals

Interview questionnaire   a questionnaire designed to be read out to the respondent by the researcher

Interview schedule   a series of questions, along with supplementary notes, devised before an interview, to remind the researcher of the questions to be asked

Interview, structured   an interview in which the researcher tries to control its pace, structure and content, frequently by using pre-planned questions

Interview, unstructured   an interview in which the researcher deliberately leaves the respondent the freedom to change the pace, structure and content of the interview

Key informant   a respondent who is selected by the researcher on the assumption that he or she possesses significant insights into, or knowledge of, the research topic

Law   a statement of the apparent empirical relationship between two or more variables

Leading question   a question in a research instrument which, by its formulation, encourages a particular answer

Life history   an approach to research which uses as data the personal, subjective accounts of people's lives

Macro level   research which focuses on large-scale events, phenomena or organisations. Research focused on smaller, individual events, or on small-scale human interaction, can be described as being at the micro level

Mean   the average value of a set of measurements, calculated by adding the set of values, and dividing the total by the number of values

Median   the median of a set of data is calculated by arranging the data in order of magnitude; the median is the size of the middle term

Methodology   the general term used to describe the process, or study, of methods of collecting, recording and analysing data

Mode   the mode of a set of data is the most common numerical value

Multiple methods   the use of a variety of data-collection methods and analysis in a research study, in order to try to construct a more comprehensive picture of the research topic

Nominal data   data which consists of placing individual instances into named categories or groups

Non-probability sample   a general approach to sampling in which there is no planned probability of an individual being included in the population sample. It is extremely difficult to generalise from a non-probability sample

Observation studies   a general term for data collection involving systematic observation. Data may involve the recording of the numbers and types of interaction between people, or the keeping of a field diary

Official record   data which consists of the formal records of businesses, government departments or organisations. It may consist of such documents as minutes of meetings or memoranda

Oral history   a method of data collection which involves interviewing people about events which they have personally experienced

Ordinal data   data which consists of placing entities in order of magnitude, but where the difference between them is unknown

Organisational research   research which investigates aspects of the social systems of organisations

Participant observation   observational research in which the researcher adopts an active role in the social setting under investigation

Personal document   data consisting of the types of document typically collected by an individual. It might include, for example, financial records or legal documents

Pilot study   a preliminary study designed to gain information to help improve the data-collection process. The term is often used in relation to piloting a questionnaire, for example

Policy research   a research study which is designed to provide data to help with the generation of policy, typically at governmental or organisational level

Population   the total number of individuals or instances to which it is intended that a research study will apply. It is often not possible to collect data from the whole population, in which case a sample is used

Positivism   an approach to data collection and analysis in the social sciences which adopts the philosophical position of the natural sciences, such as physics and chemistry, e.g. with regard to the assumption that social phenomena are measurable

Post-coding   the process of classifying qualitative data after it has been collected

Postal survey   a survey conducted by sending self-completion questionnaires through the post

Pre-coding   the classification of possible responses to a data-collection instrument before it is administered

Primary data data which is collected by the researcher for the specific purpose of a research project

Probability sample a sample in which each member of the study population has a known chance of being included

Qualitative data data which is in the form of words, either written or spoken. Such data might include tape recordings of interviews, diaries, field notes, and some types of questionnaire responses

Quantitative data data which is in the form of numbers. Such data might include psychometric test scores, some types of questionnaire responses, assessment scores, and some kinds of sociometric data

Random sample a sample whose members are selected one by one, by chance, from all the members of the study population

Ratio data data arranged in order of magnitude, where the numerical difference between values is known, and where there is an absolute zero

Reliability a data-collection instrument is reliable if the same responses are collected on two separate occasions

Respondent an individual who provides data

Respondent anonymity the ethical issue of not disclosing the identity of a respondent

Response rate the percentage of data-collection instruments which are returned by respondents

Reviewer when an article is submitted to an academic journal, it is sent by the editor to a reviewer asking for an opinion on its suitability for publication

Sample the proportion of a study population from which data is gathered

Scattergram a graphical representation of the relationship between two variables

Secondary data data which has been collected for one purpose, but is then used for a different research study

Self-completion questionnaire a questionnaire designed to be completed by the respondent, without the presence of the researcher

Snowball sample a procedure in which initial respondents are asked to name others who may be of help as respondents

Social sciences the disciplines concerned with the study of people, e.g. psychology and sociology, as opposed to the natural sciences, e.g. physics and chemistry

Software a computer package. In research, computer software is increasingly used for analysing data

Sponsor a person or organisation who provides financial support for research

Standard deviation for a set of data, this is a measure of the extent to which individual values are spread from the mean

Stratified random sample a sampling procedure in which the population is divided into predetermined sections and a random sample drawn from each

Structured observation observational research in which the researcher has carefully defined data to collect. An example would be a sociometric study

Survey a research approach in which data is collected in a systematic way (e.g. by using a questionnaire) from, usually, a relatively large sample

Systematic sample a sampling approach in which the members of a population are listed according to a criterion unconnected with the research. The researcher then selects individuals at specified intervals in the list

Transcript the written form of a tape recording of an interview

Triangulation the use of more than one data-collection method in a research investigation, in order to gain a greater understanding of the research problem

Validity a measuring instrument is valid if it actually measures what it claims to measure

Variable a characteristic of the subject of the research which has a fluctuating value

FURTHER READING

Anderson, D S and Biddle, B J (eds), *Knowledge and Policy*, London, Falmer, 1991.

Anderson, G, *Fundamentals of Educational Research*, Basingstoke, Falmer, 1990.

Armstrong, P F, 'Qualitative Strategies in Social and Educational Research: The Life History Method in Theory and Practice', *Newland Papers*, No. 14, p.8, The University of Hull, 1987.

Black, T R, *Evaluating Social Science Research*, London, Sage, 1993.

Bryman, A, *Quantity and Quality in Social Research*, London, Routledge, 1988.

Bryman, A and Cramer, D, *Quantitative Data Analysis for Social Scientists*, London, Routledge, 1994.

Burgess, R G (ed), *Field Research: A Sourcebook and Field Manual*, London, Allen and Unwin, 1982.

Burgess, R G, *Research Methods*, Walton-on-Thames, Nelson, 1993.

Cohen, L and Manion, L, *Research Methods in Education*, London, Routledge, 1989.

Creswell, J W, *Research Design*, Thousand Oaks, Sage, 1994.

Frey, J H and Oishi, S M, *How to Conduct Interviews by Telephone and in Person*, Thousand Oaks, Sage, 1995.

Gill, J and Johnson, P, *Research Methods for Managers*, London, Paul Chapman, 1991.

Glaser, B and Strauss, A L, *The Discovery of Grounded Theory*, Chicago, Aldine, 1967.

Hakim, C, *Research Design*, London, Allen and Unwin, 1987.

Hopkins, D, *A Teacher's Guide to Classroom Research*, Buckingham, Open University Press, 1993.

Hughes, J, *The Philosophy of Social Research*, London, Longman, 1980.

Kane, E, *Doing Your Own Research*, London, Marion Boyars, 1985.

Lewins, F, *Social Science Methodology*, Melbourne, Macmillan, 1992.

Macdonald, K and Tipton, C, 'Using Documents', in Gilbert, N (ed), *Researching Social Life*, London, Sage, 1995.

Mann, P H, *Methods of Social Investigation*, Oxford, Blackwell, 1985.

Marshall, C and Rossman, G B, *Designing Qualitative Research*, Newbury Park, Sage, 1989.

May, T, *Social Research*, Buckingham, Open University Press, 1993.

Oppenheim, A N, *Questionnaire Design, Interviewing and Attitude Measurement*, London, Pinter, 1992.

Porter, L R. and Coggin, W, *Research Strategies in Technical Communication*, New York, John Wiley, 1995.

Powney, J and Watts, M, *Interviewing in Educational Research*, London, Routledge and Kegan Paul, 1987.

Reason, P, 'Reflections', in Reason, P (ed), *Human Inquiry in Action*, London, Sage, 1988.

Sanger, J, *The Compleat Observer?* London, Falmer, 1996.

Sayer, A, *Method in Social Science*, London, Routledge, 1993.

Schutt, R K, *Investigating the Social World*, Thousand Oaks, Pine Forge Press, 1996.

Stringer, E T, *Action Research*, Thousand Oaks, Sage, 1996.

Weitzman, E A and Miles, M B, *Computer Programs for Qualitative Data Analysis*, Thousand Oaks, Sage, 1995.

Yin, R K, *Case Study Research*, Newbury Park, Sage, 1989.

INDEX

Other related titles

ty TEACH YOURSELF

WRITING
ESSAYS & REPORTS

PAUL OLIVER

*The daunting blank page, the chewed-up pen,
the cold sweat – when the pressure's on, what should
you do to meet your deadline with a brilliant and
well-polished essay?*

Teach Yourself Writing Essays & Reports is the book
for all students that will help you write first class
assignments at college and university. An experienced
university tutor, Paul Oliver tells you about the
conventions that will help you structure your ideas into
essays, seminar papers, research studies, reports and
portfolios. He shows you how to avoid plagiarism and
jargon, how to write an introduction and a conclusion,
and how to construct a bibliography. There is a section on
editing, and advice on how to get help from your own
tutor.